Indian Companion
to
Joseph Conrad

Indian Companion to Joseph Conrad

Mallikarjun Patil

AUTHORSPRESS
Publishers of Scholarly Books

Worldwide Circulation through Authorspress Global Network
First Published 2011
by
Authorspress
E-35/103, Jawahar Park
Laxmi Nagar, Delhi-110 092
e-mail: authorspress@yahoo.com

Indian Companion to Joseph Conrad
ISBN 978-81-7273-540-1

Printed in India at Tarun Offset, Delhi.

Preface

Joseph Conrad is one of the best twentieth century English writers. He is a great sea novelist and short story writer. He is a different and difficult writer altogether. There are many paradoxes in his life. For example, he was born a Pole and got British citizenship. He was for half of his life a seaman-captain, and then he switched over to a challenging writing career. He had an immense sea-experience and he wrote in a language which was not his own. He is the only writer who has stayed in all pa(o)rts of the world. So he reminds us of Marco Polo and V. S. Naipaul in our times. Conrad wrote entirely different kind of fiction—imperialist, modernist and partly political.

The present critical monograph on Conrad is like an Indian writers's revisiting of Conrad. The book has four chapters. Chapter I is about Conrad's life and works. Chapter II deals with a critical analysis of Conrad's entire corps of novels. Chapter II analyses his short stories; and chapter IV is about his world-view.

The present monograph on Conrad is primarily meant for Indian readers. It aims at introducing Conrad to them for a better and easier appreciation of him; the Pole, the Captain, the English writer and the thinker.

Mallikarjun Patil

Introduction

Rudyard Kipling and Joseph Conrad are treated as great colonial writers of England. If Kipling wrote supreme stories about the sea, Conrad wrote supreme stories about the sea. Conrad also reminds us of the great American sea-novelists: Herman Melville and Ernst Hemingway.

Alexander Sanders thinks that Joseph Conrad is a different kind of outsider in search of integrity in England. As a Pole he got British citizenship in 1886, and his betrayal of homeland haunts him in his writings. His writing can be diasporic and about modern man's dislocation. As a writer in exile and a writer of sea-stories of the Far East and the Pacific, he drove our attention. He also wrote political fiction. His themes develop, broaden and open up in the larger world beyond the confined, masculine world of the ship. In a dense the sea-story, *"The Secret Sharer"* (1909), the narrator speaks disarmingly of the 'great security of the sea as compared with the unrest of the land' and of a shipboard life which presents no disquieting problems. His descriptions of ship life suggest a relatively ordered society which is, by its very nature, prepared to face the challenges of an external and impersonal hostility. The ship also contains a small hierarchical society in which individual decision and responsibility take on the moral force of paramount virtue.

Andrew Sanders observes, "Conrad's tales concerned with the nature and effects of European imperialism, both economic and colonial, are of a different order to Kipling's. Conrad deals not with the multiple confrontations of India, but with the intrusion and interference of Europeans in the Pacific, in the East Indies, in South America, and in Africa. His colonizers are drawn from a variety of national backgrounds; most are disreputable, incomprehending, intolerant, and exploitative. The title character in *Lord Jim* (1900) may have proved himself a successful colonial agent and have earned himself the title of Tuan (Lord) from his grateful subjects, but his organizing virtues are seen as countered by the lasting memory of the corruption of his predecessor and by the deception and ruthless European piracy of Gentleman Brown. In Conrad's work colonialism generally emerges as both brutal and brutalizing, alienating native and settler alike. "Power is not simply corrupting, it is systematically open to abuse."

Conrad's story An Outpost of Progress (1898) indicates that the 'darkness' corrupts both internally and externally, an idea which reaches its apogee in Heart of Darkness (1899, 1902), a narrative which gradually unveils, layer by layer, an underlying horror. Imperialism is initially expounded as a variety of brutish idealism. There is no redemption from 'the buying and selling gang which bosses the rotten show. Nostromo (1904) (a title which implies the presence of 'our man') is concerned with silver, insurrection, and external interference in an unstable South American republic.

Andrew Sanders observes, "Conrad's gentlemanly Polish background, and his diverse professional and intellectual interests, made for ambiguities which run through his life and work. Having been born an unwilling subject of the Russian Tsar, and having accepted exile from nationalist politics and his native language, he steadily explores and interrelates themes of guilt and dislocation." In *Under Western Eyes* (1911) he writes directly about the dangerous instabilities of society under the Russian autocracy, but his own antipathy to Russia and to things Russian renders it a somewhat wayward response to an obviously Dostoevskyan precedent. The novel's wandering narrator, an elderly English teacher of languages in Geneva, draws both on his experience of the exiled Russian student Kirylo Sidorovitch Razumov and on Razumov's diary. Razumov (whose name is derived from the Russian term 'son of reason') is a double exile in Switzerland; he has betrayed a revolutionary fellow-student to the Tsar's police, and, as his guilt remains concealed, he is acting out a lie of heroic virtue amongst a group of alienated expatriates. The narrator observes all with foreign, 'western' eyes, eyes which only partially grasp the import of Razumov's pressing need for confession and expiation. *The Secret Agent* (1907), in some ways a far more assured and far more disturbing novel, is also concerned with revolution and revolutionaries, unflatteringly observed in a murky, seedy, untidy London. In some telling ways the novel looks back both to Dickens and to the sensation fiction of the 1860s, but it also conveys a distinctly modern sense of alienation, disquiet, and dislocation. The central character, Verloc, an agent provocateur in the employ of a 'foreign' (but almost certainly Russian) embassy, is required by his ambassadorial handler to commit a terrorist act of 'shocking senselessness' and 'gra-tuitous blasphemy' by blowing up the Greenwich Meridian.

The present book has four chapters. Chapter 1 is about Conrad's life and works. Chapter 2 is a critical, yet brief analysis of his great novels *Almayer's Folly* (1895), *The Nigger of the 'Narcissus'* (1897), *Heart of Darkness* (1902), *Lord Jim* (1900), *Typhoon'* (1903), *Nostromo* (1904), *Under the Western Eyes* (1911), *Chance* (1913) and *Victory* (1915). On the other hand, *An Outcast of the Islands* (1896), *The Secret Agent* (1907), *Freya of the Seven Isles* (1902), *The Shadow Line* (1917), *The Arrow of Gold* (1919), *The Rescue* (1920), *The Rover* (1923), *Suspense* (1925) and *The Sisters* (1928) are his minor novels. In fact, *The Suspense* and *The Sisters* remained incomplete.

Chapter 3 is about Conrad's short stories. As we know Conrad, like many other contemporary writers, wrote short stories for magazines. He wanted both money and popularity. He published six books of short stories, *Tales of Unrest* (1898), *Youth: A Narrative and Two Other Stories* (1902), *A Set of Six* (1908), *'Twist Land and Sea* (1912), and *Within the Tides* (1915). His *Tales of Hearsay* (1925) appeared posthumously. His stories like "An Outpost of Progress," "The Lagoon," "Youth," "The End of the Tether," "Typhoon," "Falk," "A Smile of Fortune," "The Secret Sharer" and "Prince Roman" attracted a wide range of audience.

The last chapter deals with Conrad's worldview. It has items like Conrad, and Poland, imperialism, Modernism, Schopenhauer, Nietzsche, Rousseau, Dickens, Hardy and others. Details about his problems of language and his vision of life are discussed. In brief, the book aims at introducing Conrad to Indian readers.

Mallikarjun Patil

Contents

1 Joseph Conard's Life and Works

Joseph Conrad is a great novelist of the twentieth century English literature. He was born to Apollo Natecz Korzeniowski and mother Evalina Bobrowska in Derebczynka Manor near Berdyczow in the Ukraine. He was an orphan, a Pole, Catholic, nobleman, etc. Later he became an expatriate at the age of 17, sailor, gun-runner, attempted suicide, naturalized Englishman, master mariner in the British Merchant Navy, Captain of a Cango river-steamer and eventually an English novelist. Henry James would say to him, "No one has *known*–for intellectual use–the things you know."

Then Conrad's Poland was dominated by Russia. The Conrad nobility rebelled against this domination in 1794 and 1830. The Korezeniowskis, because of political confrontation, lost their estates, while the Bobrowskis followed a policy of appeasement and saved themselves. Conrad's uncle Thaddeus Bobrowski, often counselled Conrad against rebellion. He said, "I see with pleasure that the Nateez [father's family] in you has been modified under the influence of the Bobroszczaki [mother's family]...This time I rejoice over the influence of my family, although I don't in the least deny that the Nateczes have a spirit of initiative and enterprise greater than that which is in my blood."

Evalina Bobrowska and Apollo Korzenioski first met in 1847 and fell in love with each other. But Eva's father opposed their marriage because Appollo neither worked hard, nor owned any property. But once Eva's father died, the two married. Thaddeus described Apollo as "violent in emotions...unpractical in his deeds, often helpless and unresourceful," and in three years Apollo, having exhausted his wife's dowry, devoted himself to politics and writing. During much of the remainder of his life he was supported by members of his wife's family.

On 3 December 1857 at Berdyzów (Ukrainian Berdichev) in Podolia, Conrad was born, their first and only child, and christened Józef Teodor Konrad Korzeniowski. Teodor and Józef were the names of his grandfathers, and Konrad seems to have come from the hero of the famous poem *Konrad Wallenrod* by the Romantic poet and dramatist Mickiewicz.

In the spring of 1859, Apollo went to try his luck and his literary talents at Zytomierz, then the intellectual centre of the province. He had already written two satirical comedies and some poems reflecting his patriotism and social radicalism, and had translated Victor Hugo from the French; he now established a new literary fortnightly. Then he moved to Warsaw for further adventure, while Eva lived in Ukarine.

"Konrad grows up beautifully. He has a heart of gold, and with his conscience and intellect there won't be any difficulty with you working for his future," Eva wrote to her husband. At the beginning of October 1861, she and Conrad joined Apollo in Warsaw. Their home, not surprisingly, had become a meeting place for adherents to the cause of Polish nationalism, and Apollo was involved in underground political activity. His passionate and patriotic allegiance to Poland is expressed in this poem commemorating his son's baptism: "My child, my son, if the enemy called you a nobleman and a Christian—tell yourself that you are a pagan and that your nobility is rot...My child, my son—tell yourself that you are without land, without love, without Fatherland, without humanity—as long as Poland, our Mother, is enslaved." On 21 October Apollo was arrested on the ground of insurgency. In fact, the whole family was imprisoned.

The Conrads were sentenced to settlement in a distant province, and in May 1862, escorted by two policemen, left for exile in Vologda in northern Russia, arriving in June. Both Conrad and Eva were ill on the way. The family spent a miserable year there. Several relatives died during a new period of Russian repression, and Eva was now suffering from tuberculosis. Apollo wrote to a friend: "Vologda is a great three-verst marsh... everything rotting and shifting under one's feet....The climate consists of two seasons of the year: a white winter and a green winter. The white winter lasts nine and a half months and the green one two and a half. We are now at the onset of the green winter: it has already been raining ceaselessly for twenty one days....The population is a nightmare: disease-ridden corpses."

The following summer, thanks to the intervention of friends, the family were allowed to move to Chernikhov.

Appolo translated Hugo Dicknes and Shakeseare, and wrote his anti-Russian memoirs, *Poland and Muscovy,* but Eva was dying. Apollo confided to his friend Kazimierz Kaszweski: 'nostalgia and the repeated blows falling on our families have been slowly killing my wife.... Our little Konrad is inevitably neglected,' and on 18 April 1865, when Conrad was seven, his mother died. His father did not mask despair: "Should I describe this place I would say that on one side it is bounded by locked doors behind which the being dearest to me breathed her last, without my being able to wipe even the death sweat from her brow, while on the other...I see what Dante did *not* describe...."

For the next three years, Conrad was to live a strange, isolated life, coloured by his father's grief and bitterness. Apollo referred to him as 'my poor little orphan.' During this period, Conrad spent one holiday with his uncle Thaddeus, finding companionship of his own age in Thaddeus's daughter Józefa; and later, because of illness, he was taken by his grandmother to Kiev for medical advice.

Apollo was ill in 1867, and he was allowed to stay in Lvov, where the boy attended school. They moved to Carlow in 1869. Later Conrad wrote of his bad days: "I don't know what would have become of me if I had not been a reading boy. My prep finished I would have had nothing to do but sit and watch the awful stillness of the sick room flow out through the closed door and coldly enfold my scared heart.... I looked forward to what was coming with an incredulous terror. I turned my eyes from it sometimes with success, and yet all the time I had an awful sensation of the inevitable. I had also moments of revolt which stripped off me some of my simple trust in the government of the universe."

Conrad's father burnt down his manuscripts and passed away on 23 May 1869. This reminds us of Franz Kafka's sad literary career a few decades later.

Thirty years later, Conrad described his father as having 'great sensibilities' and an 'exalted and dreamy temperament; with a terrible gift of irony and of gloomy disposition.' 'My father,' he insisted, 'was simply a patriot....'

Uncle Thaddeus looked after the young Conrad now. Thaddeus was exactly opposite to Apollo. He called Conrad's father a sentimentalist. He was the type of benevolent guardian figure that Conrad dealt with in the character of Stein in Lord Jim and Captain Lingard in the Bornean stories.

Conrad was first placed in a boarding-house in Cracow; and a medical student, Adam Marek Pulman, was chosen to be his private tutor. His grandmother stayed in Cracow from 1870 to 1873 to take care of the boy, but in September 1873 he was sent to a boarding-house in Lvov run by a distant relative, Antoni Syroczyñski. It seems likely that Conrad was at odds with his environment at this time, and was felt to be getting out of hand.

Apparently, while he was at Lvov, Conrad fell in love, either with Tekla Syroczyñska or with Janina Taube, the sisters of his friends. He said later that Antonia Avellanos in Nostromo was modelled on his first love.

Conrad had told his uncle Thaddeus in 1872 that he wished to go to sea. Thaddeus's shock 'could not have been greater if I had announced the intention of entering a Carthusian monastery,' Conrad recalled. His ambition caused 'a wave of scandalized astonishment.' 'People wondered what Mr. T.B. would do now with his worrying nephew.' In 1874, Thaddeus agreed to send him off to the Merchant Marine.

Norman Sherry writes, "Certainly Thaddeus had tried in vain to secure him Austrian citizenship, but just as certainly the question why Conrad left his homeland cannot be fully answered. Years later, in A *Personal Record,* Conrad raised that mysterious question; 'Why should I...undertake the pursuit of fantastic meals of salt junk and hard tack upon the wide seas? ...The part of the inexplicable should be allowed for in appraising the conduct of men in a world where no explanation is final.' In any case, in October 1874, Conrad left Poland for Marseilles, with introductions arranged and a reasonable amount of money 2,000 francs a year in monthly instalments. Behind him already was more tragic experience than is given to many men in a lifetime: he was moved by the unlikely impulse, for a native of a land-locked country, to become a seaman; and, not yet seventeen, he was stepping alone into a new existence. This action, in its essentials, was to become a characteristic one of Conrad at intervals during his life."

Conrad was to spend four years in France and, at least initially, it must have seemed to the young man of seventeen that all his desires were being fulfilled. As 'le petiti ami de Baptistin', he was made guest of the Corporation of Pilots, and had the freedom of their boats and homes night and day.

Conrad was to travel in the ships of M.Delestang, who supported Don Carlos de Bourbon's royalist cause for the Spanish throne. Then he loved to stay at Marseilles as his biography Jean Aubry writes. Conrad began his career as a seaman. Two months after his arrival in Marseilles, he made his first voyage –as a passenger– to Martinique in the *Mont Blanc,* and on her next visit to the West Indies on 25 June 1875. He was listed as an apprentice.

He returned to Marseilles in December 1875 and spent the following six months there. He would seem at this time to have devoted himself to enjoying life in the port, and he certainly spent a good deal of money. In his "Document," Thaddeus set down an account of Conrad's extravagances. Conrad's money difficulties, which plagued him all his life, had begun.

On 8 July 1876, Conrad sailed again to the West Indies, this time as a steward on the *Saint-Antoine*–a memorable voyage for him, for the first mate was certain Corsican called Dominic Cervoni, a man of forty-two who was to impress Conrad greatly at the time and to figure, later on, in *The Mirror of the Sea* and *Nostromo*. There was another 15-year-old seaman, Cesar Cervoni. The period from March 1877 to February 1878 was to form the climax of Conrad's experience in Marseilles.

Conrad was prevented from sailing again in the Saint-Antoine in March 1877 because of an anal abscess, and on excuse that he was later to make a world voyage in this ship, Conrad obtained another 3,000 fancs from Thaddeus. He had quarrelled with M. Delestang, and now considered transferring to the British Merchant Navy, or seeking help from the Japanese Consul in joining the Japanese Navy. From the autumn of 1877 until February 1878, Thaddeus concluded that Conrad was voyaging in the *Saint Antoine*. Conrad's *The Mirror of the Sea* and *The Arrow of Gold* later suggested that he was in fact involved in a highly dangerous venture with a smuggling syndicate organized by a woman called Rita de Lastaola. Conrad, Dominic Cervoni and Cesear Cervoni were supposedly smuggling arms into Spain for the Carlist cause on the *Tremolino*. The ship was ultimately sunk to prevent capture. Later, Conrad told his wife that 'he and the other smugglers had hidden for days in a low posada, in an underground cellar that was more like a cavern, till the authorities had given up the search.' Conrad, supposedly in love with Rita, many years later wrote to Sir Sidney Colvin that those '*42-year-old episodes*' still brought 'a slight tightness of the chest'. *The Arrow of Gold* suggests that he fought a duel over Doña Rita and was wounded.

Conrad borrowed 800 francs and went to Villefranche to join the American naval service. Failing in this, he tried his luck at Monte Carlo and lost his 800 francs. He returned to Marseilles, invited the man who had loaned him the money to tea, but before he arrived made an attempt to shoot himself. Taking stock of the situation in Marseilles, Thaddeus recorded that he paid out another 3,000 francs to clear Conrad's debts and noted that his nephew did not drink, or gamble; that his manners were good; that he was popular with the seamen and captains; and that he seemed a skilled sailor. Later, his uncle, who never feared treading on corns, was to tell Conrad: 'You were idling for nearly a whole year—you fell into debt, you deliberately shot yourself.' It was clearly time to leave Marseilles, and Conrad made a second leap into the unknown.

Now Conrad joined the English Merchant Marine. So far hed had stayed in France for four years. He sailed in the British ship Mavis, coal freighter bound first for Constantinople and then for Lowestoft, where she arrived on 18 June 1878.

For Madox Ford, Conrad's later friend and collaborator, helps to place the significance at that time of what Thaddeus called 'the misty shores of hospitable Albion': "During the last century if you went down to Tilbury Dock you would see families of Jewish-Poland emigrants landing. As soon they landed they fell on their hands and knees and kissed the soil of the land of Freedom...England...and immense power standing for liberty and hospitality for refugees; vigilant over a pax Britannica that embraced the world.... Conrad was a Pole of the last century [and he] could ask nothing better."

Conrad's misdemeanour on this occasion lay in quarrelling with the captain of the *Mavis* on the return journey from Constantinople. He then went to London and spent most of his money. He found another ship, the *Skimmer of the Seas,* a coaster running between Lowestoft and Newscastle.

Norman Sherry writes, "From the year 1878 when he was twenty to the year 1894 when he was thirty-six, Joseph Conrad was a restless, adventurous, merchant seaman, with the emphasis upon the restlessness. He began the period as a young foreigner with very little English, with a dreamy expression and a hint of determination in his eyes, if his portrait of 1873 is an accurate one. He was M. George of *The Arrow of Gold,* with impeccable manners and a capacity for going through money quickly. He was Decoud of *Nostromo,* cosmopolitan and cynical. He was still Jozef Teodor Konrad Korzeniowski. He ended the period in 1896, as photographs show, as a bearded sea captain, with a stern glance and a lined face, a man of vast experience and broken health, with a strong foreign accent, with no great success in his present career, but as Joseph Conrad the novelist, who had published in England his first novel, *Almayer's Folly.*"

Writing later of his earliest experience in England he said: "...the North Sea was my finishing school of seamanship before I launched myself on the wider oceans..... My class-room was the region of the English East Coast which, in the year of Peace with Honour, had long forgotten the war episodes belonging to its maritime history...My teachers had been the sailors of the Norfolk shore; coast men, with steady eyes, mighty limbs, and gentle voice...each built as through to last for ever, and coloured like a Christmas Card. Tan and pink-gold hair and blue eyes—with that Northern straight away there look!"

His search was successful: on 12 October 1878 he embarked as an ordinary seaman on a wool-clipper, the *Duke of Sutherland,* bound for Australia. Conrad moved steadily after this through the various stages of seamanship, obtaining his second mate's ticket in 1880; his first mate's in 1884; and his master's in 1886. 'I have been face to face at various times with all examiners of the Port London, in my generation....' His uncle Thaddeus was equally delighted: 'First, dear Sir, you have proved to our country and your own people that you have not eaten your bread in the world for four years in vain; secondly, that you have succeeded in overcoming the difficulties that arise from the language itself, and from your difficult position as a foreigner without any patronage to support you.... Now we need work and endurance, endurance and work....' And when Conrad obtained his Master's certificate: 'Long live the "Ordin. Master in the British merchant Service"!!

But these successes were accompanied by failures and discontents and restlessness, which, when reported to Thaddeus, aroused in him puzzlement, anger and anxiety at different times. Conrad, for example, does not appear to have stayed long with any ship, frequently because he quarrelled with the captain. He was restless, rather quarrelling, and a spendthrift. Further he would try to earn extra money, say by whaling or smuggling. Thaddeus always scotched such idea: 'You would not be a Natecz, dear boy, if you were steady in your enterprises and if you didn't chase after ever new projects'; 'Since you are a Natecz, bcware of risky speculations based only on hope; for your grandfather squandered all his property speculatig, and your Uncle...got into debt...and died heavily in debt.'

It was after leaving the Europa that Conrad met two men whose friendship for him was to last many years. In 1880, at the offices of a shipping agent, he was introduced to G. F.W. Hope, a company director who had once sailed, as had Conrad, in the *Duke of Sutherland*. The two men went into the London tavern for lunch, and Hope recalls Conrad's 'very broken English.' Hope saw Conrad afterwards whenever he returned from a voyage, and heard of his experiences and plans. Later he befriended A.P. Krieger who helped Conrad for naturalization. After sailing in the wool-clipper *Loch Etive* to Sydney and returning in her via the Cape Horn route in April 1881, Conrad found a berth as second mate on the fated barque *Palestie*, bound for Bangkok. It was a momentous voyage in many ways, described later by Conrad in his story *Youth*. At last, the *Palestine* cleared for Bangkok. She was 'all rust, dust, grime,' 'heavy with age' and she 'wallowed on the Atlantic like an old candle-box.' "But trouble did not come to the vessel until she was east of the Bangka Strait when her cargo of coal caught fire." This trip facilitated Conrad for a view of the East, and later inspired him for literature.

The Inquiry into the loss of *Palestine* was held in Singapore and attended by Conrad, and a reflection of it can most certainly be seen in the Inquiry into the loss of the Patna in the novel *Lord Jim*. On returning to England in May 1883, Conrad went off for a long-planned meeting with his uncle, the first in almost ten years. They stayed at Marienbad and then at Toplitz where the young sea-man, now twenty-five, was photographed.

He left his next ship—the *Riversdale*, a sailing ship of 1,500 tons, bound for the East—at Madra, and returned home in another sailing-ship the *Narcissus*, which he joined at Bombay. She was 'a lovely ship, with all the graces of a yacht', and as second mate he sailed in her to Dunkirk. This ship and her voyage formed the basis for *The Nigger of the 'Narcissus.'* Though Conrad denied that James Wait, the nigger of the story was one of the Narcissus's crew, he conceded, 'Most of the personages I portrayed actually belonged to the crew of the real *'Narcissus.'* The story is Conrad's masterpiece of the sea.

It was on this occasion, according to Hope, that for the first and only time Conrad brought a pet from abroad—a monkey which tore up a lot of important papers in Krieger's office at Barr, Moering & Co., and had to be 'disposed of...to a Jew in the Minories.'

Conrad's next voyage to the Far East was the *Tilkhurst* which sailed from Hull in April 1885. While she was coaling at Cardiff Conrad met Spiridion Kliszczewski, son of a Polish immigrant and watch maker, and became friendly with him, a friendship which lasted for some years. Conrad wrote letters to this man first time in English.

In 1887, Conrad's fourth and final, but the longest and the most fruitful visit to the Far East began when he signed as first mate on the *Highland Forest*. She was bound for Samarang in Java, and he joined her in Amsterdam. Conrad was chief mate for the first time and the fact of his elevation kept him warm. Since the captain had not yet arrived, Conrad was in charge of stowing the cargo. It was after loading was complete that stranger in a black bowler and a short drab overcoat appeared on the quay—the captain, John Mc-Whirr. *Typhoon* is about him.

Norman Sherry observes, "During the *Highland Forest's* 'lively' passage, her chief mate's back was injured by a flying spar, and he became subject to 'inexplicable periods of powerlessness, sudden accesses mysterious pain.' A Dutch doctor in Samarang expressed his fears: 'Ah, friend, you are young yet; it may be very serious for your whole life. You must leave your ship; you must quite silent be for three months.' On the advice of the doctor Conrad was shipped to Singapore, where he entered hospital. The material for his later Eastern novels was all about him; the foundations of his next career were being laid. Singapore was to be the 'great Eastern port' of *Lord Jim, The End of the Tether, The Rescue and the Shadow-Line.*"

Conrad liked Singapore very much. 'The East, and especially Singapore, was peopled with men who appear in Conrad's fiction. Augustus Podmore Williams, a ship chandler's water-clerk in the port, had been mate of the pilgrim ship *Jeddah* which sailed from Singapore in 1880 and was abandoned by her European officers after a storm, leaving 1,000 Moslem pilgrims to their doom. The captain cabled from Aden that their ship had foundered and all the pilgrims had perished, but the following day the *Jeddah* was towed into Aden harbour by the Antenor with all the pilgrims safe on board. This scandal was the source of *Lord Jim*.

In August, Conrad, now discharged from hospital, decided against returning to England, and was taken on as mate of the steamship *Vidar*, whose captain, Craig, told Jean-Aubry that he first met Conrad 'at the shipping-Office of Singapore about the middle of August 1887': 'He pleased me at once by his manners, which were distinguished and reserved.' The *Vidar* was a local ship, owned by an Arab called Syed Mohsin Bin Saleh A1 Joffree, who was well known and liked in Singapore. As Conrad wrote: 'He was head of a great House of Strains Arabs, but as loyal a subject of the complex British Empire as you could find east of the Suez Canal...he had a great occult power amongst his own people.' The *Vidar* traded among the islands of the South-East Asian archipelago, and Conrad stayed with her four and a half months, repeating the journey as it is described in *The Shadow-Line* and *The End of the Tether*. As part of the journey, the *Vidar* travelled up the Berau River in Borneo, and here Conrad discovered another area that was to be a fruitful source for his later novels. It was here that Conrad first met Chalres Olmeijer, who was to become his scapegoat hero, Almayer. It was here also that Conrad learnt of the influence of Captain William Lingard, who had surveyed the Berau and had a channel named after him in the charts, who had fought pirates and was known as the 'Rajah Laut'

(King of the Seas) by the Malays, who established Olmeijer (and later his nephew Jim Lingard) at the trading post at Tandjong Redeb, and another nephew, Joshua, in Singapore. Captain Lingard owned the *Coeran*, the *West Indian* and the *Rajah Laut*, and a local newspaper described him as 'a personage of almost mythical renown, a sort of ubiquitous sea-hero, perhaps at times a sort of terror to evildoers, all over Eastern waters form Singapore to Torres Straits, and from Timor to Mindanao.' He finally returned to England, and died in Ashton near Macclesfied. William Lingard became, in recognizable form, the Captain Tom Lingard of Conrad's early Eastern novels and of *The Rescue*.

On 4 January 1888, Conrad, again unpredictably, gave up his berth on *Vidar*, and there began that series of events leading up to his first—and only—command, which he chronicled, with some imaginative distortion, in *The Shadow-Line*. It was the Master Attendant of Singapore, Captain Ellis, who gave Conrad command of a small barque, the *Otago*, then in Bangkok. The *Otago* had been built in Glasgow in 1869, she was 367 tons gross, and whatever troubles he had initially in taking her over, Conrad always spoke of her with affection: 'my first command... sure of tenderly remembered existence as long as I live.' The *Otaga*, after much delay, at last left for her journey of 800 miles down the gulf of Siam to Singapore, a journey which took there and which was dogged by sickness.

After this nightmarish voyage, the *Otago* went on to Sydney, arriving there on 7 May: 'Arrivals—May 7 *Otago*, barque, 347 tons. Captain Konkorentowski [*sic*] from Bangkok' (*Sydney Morning Herald*). Conrad remained with this ship, sailing next to Mauritius where he spent three weeks. By chance, we have quite a lot of information about those three weeks. There is, to begin with, a description, by one of the ship's charterers, of Conrad's appearance at the age of thirty-one, which shows that Conrad the seaman was still conscious of his Polish heritage: "...Captain Korzeniowski was always dressed with great elegance. I can still see him...arriving in my office almost every day dressed in a black or dark coat, a vest that was usually light in colour, and fancy trousers; everything well cut and very stylish; on his head a black or grey derby titled slightly to one side. He invariably wore gloves and carried a cane with a gold knob.... He was not...very popular with his colleagues, who sarcastically called him 'the Russian Count."

Conrad became quite intimate with one of the French families, which he describes in "A Smile of Fortune" as 'descendants of the old colonists; all noble, all impoverished, and living a narrow domestic life in dull, dignified decay.' Now Conrad wrote his name as 'J.K.C.' He fell in love with a lady called Eugenie Renouf, but soon gave up his desire for her as she was engaged. In 1889 Conrad resigned his command. Probably his uncle had asked him to return to Poland. Conrad left Adelaide for Europe on 3 April in the *Nurenberg*. Now he was called Captain Conrad. Back in London Conrad sat in his Bessborough Gardens lodgings in London, and began to write his first novel *Almayer's Folly*. He carried the script with him to Ukraine. Now he had a chance to go to Congo, and see Africa.

This was the Congo, but Africa generally for Conrad had the heroic and adventurous attraction of the great explorers. During that summer of 1889, Africa had been very much in the news again. Henry Morton Stanley's expedition from Zanzibar to the Lower Congo took place in 1876-7; afterwards, he was employed by King Leopold of the Belgains to establish trading posts across Central Africa; and in 1889, following his successful and much publicized search for Livingstone, with its laconic climax—'Dr Livingstone, I presume'–Stanely was again in the news through his search for and relief of Emin Pash. It was against this background that Conrad made strenuous efforts to get to the Congo, and ultimately fulfilled his boyhood ambition in 'a wretched little stern-wheel steamboat...moored to the bank of an African river...Everything was dark under the stars...I have smoked a pipe of peace at midnight in the very heart of the African continent, and felt very lonely there.'

Conrad visited Poland in 1890. He met a relative writer Marguerite Poradowska. Madame Poradowska was in her early forties, and renowned for her beauty. Conrad's wife later wrote that 'she was, I think, the most beautiful woman I had ever seen.' She was also the statuesque, forceful kind of woman to whom Conrad seems to have been always attracted.

Now Conrad met his uncle Thaddeus in Kiev. The latter gave him the so called "Document." He said he spent 3,600 + 17,454 roubles for his upbringing. The uncle opposed Conrad's wish to go to Congo.

Conrad sailed in a French ship, the *Ville de Maceio,* on 10 May. In a letter he wrote: 'We left Bordeaux on a rainy day...haunting memories; vague regrets; still vaguer hopes. One is skeptical of the future.' Conrad found that many people died due to illness or encounter with Africans over ivory trade. Conrad's experience was to be humiliating, frustrating and disastrous in terms of his future health, but his sharpness of eye and recall of events when he came to write his greatest story *Heart of Darkness,* were precise and evocative. Perhaps the only good that came out of the experience was his meeting with Roger Casement at Matadi on 13 June 1890. Many years later Conrad was to describe him as having 'a touch of the Conquistador.'Casement, who in 1903 was to take part in exposing the atrocities perpetrated in the Congo, was knighted in 1911, but degraded and executed for high treason in 1916. But Conrad developed deep hatred for Delcommune, manager of the Kinchassa station and his immediate superior. Conrad's first biographer, Jean-Aubry, recalled that, from Conrad's reminiscences about the Congo, 'what remains most vividly in my mind is, first the landscape with the river wide as a sea...and second, the hostile and disagreeable figure of Delcommune.' Something of Conrad's feeling towards Delcommune is shown in a letter written from the Congo: 'The manager is a common ivory-dealer with sordid instincts who considers himself a merchant though he is only a kind of African shopkeeper.' "Going up that river' [he wrote] 'was like traveling back to the earliest beginnings of the world, when vegetation rioted on the earth and the big trees were kings.... The reaches opened before us and closed behind, as if the forest had stepped leisurely across the water to bar the way for our return. We penetrated deeper and deeper into the heart of darkness. It was very quiet there.' At the Stanley Falls station he experienced a 'profound disillusionment.' Later a crew, Klein, who as Kurtz, was buried. In *Heart of Darkness* the narrator, Marlow, tells us that Kurtz was buried in a muddy hole. After a prodigious search a missionary found and interviewed for me an old negress who recalled seventy-eight years after the event seeing Klein, Kurtz's original, being buried.

On his return to England, it was Conrad's friend, Adolf Krieger, who, seeing him half-dead with fever, arranged for the traveler to enter the German Hospital at Dalston, London. Conrad was to suffer for the rest of his life from malarial gout. From the German Hospital he went on to a hydropathic establishment in Champel, near Geneva, where he completed the eighth chapter of *Almayer's Folly,* and returned almost a month later to London, temporarily in better health.

Conrad's Congo experiences were terrible, and the same made him an intellectual and philosophical.

On his second voyage the passengers included Edward Sanderson, son of the headmaster of Elstree Preparatory School, and John Galsworthy, then a very young man just down from Oxford. Galsworthy has left us his first impression of Conrad: "He was superintending the stowage of cargo. Very dark he looked in the burning sunlight, tanned, with a peaked brown beard, almost black hair, and dark brown eyes, over which the lids were deeply folded.... He spoke to me with a strong foreign accent. He seemed to me strange on an English ship.... Ever a great teller of a tale, he had already nearly twenty years of tales to tell. Tales of ships and storms, of Polish revolution, of youthful Carlist gun-running adventure, of the Malay seas, and the Congo."

The period from 1983 to 1894 was to be of great significance in his life, though he could not then know it. In August he spent a month with his uncle in Poland, and to do this he gave up his berth on the *Torrens*. Soon after his uncle passed away.

Back in England, Conrad asked an aunt for a job either in a Suez Canal as pilot or in the Pearl fishers off the Australian coast. Then he boarded *Adowa* tc Canada and returned to London. This was Conrad's last sea-voyage, coinciding with the death of his uncle.

Now in 1894, Conrad submitted the script *Almayer's Folly* to Fisher Unwin for publication. Edward Garnett, the press adviser accepted it for £ 20 as copy right. So Conrad's days as a seaman were over.

The acceptance of *Almayer's Folly* formed a watershed in his life and brought about another change of role. The nervousness and suspicion of this 'Polish gentleman cased in British tar' at the commencement of his new career come out in his reaction on meeting his publishers: "at first the two 'readers' of the firm...complimented me effusively (were they by any chance making fun of me?)." But one of those readers, W. H. Chesson, was to recall 'how the magical melancholy of that masterpiece [*Almayer's Folly*] submerged me and how its note of haunted loneliness called me into isolation, while I read it in the clamorous heart of London.' The other reader was Edward Garnett, whose mission was 'to discover the genius and fight for his recognition.' He discovered John Galsworthy, D. H. Lawrence, W. H. Deavies, W. H. Hudson and H. E. Bates, and he was to be for a long time Conrad's friend and adviser.

Conrad's new occupation did not fundamentally alter his nature and outlook. 'His whole attitude of life was opposed to any idea of rest; he gave the impression of continual restlessness.' His wife wrote later, and a friend said, 'one always felt that there was a depth within him that even after years of the closest friendship, one had not reached.' Externally, Conrad's life changed to the extent that he married, had children, wrote his novels and made his home at various houses in southern England. His true existence was now buried within his imagination where his novels were created out of his past.

Conrad went on to write *An Outcast of the Islands*, dashing off to Switzerland to finish it, and on the publication of these first novels, *Almayer's Folly* in 1895 and *An Outcast of the Islands* in 1896, he was given a sympathetic reception by the critics. H. G. Wells reviewed the second book anonymously in the *Saturday Review* and to whom Conrad wrote, being delighted to learn his identity.

Some time between 1893 and 1894, Conrad met, through his friend G.F.W. Hope, a Miss Jessie George who was working as a 'typewriter' in the city. Their friendship developed, and early in 1895 he proposed to her. They had taken refuge from the terrible weather in the National Gallery, Jessie Conrad recalled, and Conrad said suddenly, 'Look here, my dear, we had better get married and out of this. Look at the weather. We will get married at once and get over to France. How soon can you be ready? In a week—a fortnight?' He announced that he had not very long to live and had no intention of having children. He said, "Jessie is her name; George her surname. She is small, not at all striking-looking person." They were married on 24 March 1896 at the St.

Geogre Register Office, Hanover Square, with Conrad's oldest friends in England Hope and Krieger, as witnesses.

Jessie Conrad's life with her husband was not altogether an easy one, or so her two books about him suggest, but with her placid and self-contained temperament, she was in some ways an ideal wife for a man of Conrad's genius and nature. They spent the first months of their married life on the rockyless and barren Ile-Grande near Lannion, Brittany, where Conrad began '*Narcissus*' and wrote some short stories. Jessie immediately took on her duties as typist for him. Conrad wrote the macabre *An Outpost of Progess* (A story set in the Congo), the painful *Idiots*, and the gentle Malay story *Lagoon*, which he himself described as having 'lots of second-hand Conradese in it'. He struggled ineffectively with *The Rescuer*.

Thus, in these early months of marriage, Conrad's pattern was established-difficulties in writing, bouts of crippling malarial gout and fever, fits of depression, financial difficulties, and frequent dashes to the Continent for relief.

The Conrads lived at first near their friends the Hopes at Stanford-le-Hope, Essex, in a house Conrad called 'damned jerry-built rabbit hutch.' Here Conrad finished *The Nigger of the 'Narcissus'* towards the end writing to Garnett: 'I can't eat-I dream-nightmares-and scare my wife. I wish it was over!' But the struggle was worthwhile. The novel, accepted by W. E. Henley for the *New Review* and published in book form in 1897, received what Garnett called 'a general blast of eulogy from a dozen impressive sources,' and it can be seen as marking the end of Conrad's apprenticeship as a writer.

In March 1897, the Conrads moved to an Elizabethan farmhouse, Ivy Walls, not far from their first home. Conrad went on to write Youth, which was sent to William Black-wood, publisher of *Blackwood's Magazine*, in June 1898, and he began a short story called "Jim" which was to grow into the novel *Lord Jim*.

He was under the constant pressure of having to live on what he could earn as a writer, and this pressure must have increased with the knowledge, in July 1897, that *Jessie* was pregnant.

But in terms of congenial companionship, life was improving for Conrad. Edward Garnett, John Glasworthy and Edward

Sanderson visited him, and the publication of *An Outpost of Progess* (1897) brought about a lifelong friendship with Robert Bontine Cunninghame Graham, the adventurous and romantic descendant of King Robert II of Scotland, who also had Spanish and Italian blood in his veins. Graham had spent eight years in South America, ranching and living with *gauchos*, and had prospected for gold in Spain. He was at one time an MP (Liberal), involved in the Bloody Sunday demonstration in Trafalgar Square with William Morris, Bernard Shaw, Mrs Annie Besant and Prince Kropotkin. Conrad and Cunninghame Graham had this in common—they were both adventurers, they had both wandered over great parts of the globe, both were courageous journeyers. But politically they were far apart.

Stephen Crane, author of *The Red Badge of Courage*, a book with a rigorously honest attitude to war, had first met Conrad when Sidney Pawling, of the publishers Heinemann, took them both to lunch in 1897. Afterwards the two tramped the streets of London together and once Crane stayed with the Conrads.

In September 1898, while staying with Edward Garnett, Conrad met Ford Madox Ford and seven years later such was the strength of their friendship that he was able to write to H.G. Wells: 'As to Ford he is a sort of lifelong habit.'

Ford Madox Ford (originally Hueffer), son of a famous music critic and related to both Ford Madox Brown, the painter, and William Michale Rossetti, was then twenty-four and already publishing. Wells described Ford as "a long blonde with a drawling manner...What he is really or if he is really, nobody knows now and he least of all; he has become a great system of assumed persons and dramatized selves."

Ford suggested that the Conrads should rent from him Pent Farm, an old farmhouse at Stanford, near Hythe in south-west Kent, and as Conrad liked it immediately, they moved in at beginning of autumn.

Pent Farm was their from 1898 until 1907. It was remote but by chance it was 'at the very heart of English literary life of that periods.' Henry James lived at Rye. He and Conrad were foreigners, both extremely courteous in manner, they spoke French for preference and Conrad addressed James as 'mon cher Maitre.' H. G. Wells lived at Sandgate and Rudyard Kipling at

Rottingdean. Wells and Conrad were totally different characters, and their friendship was never a close one.

The household at Pent Farm centred about Conrad who was never to be disturbed when he was writing. He would work at odd hours as the inspiration occurred, often throughout the night. He was irascible, at times, and eccentric and his temper was uncertain. Norman Sherry says, "In spite of constant shortage of money, he was one of the first in England to run a car, which he drove furiously always wearing his grey bowler hat and Havelock, with his monocle in his eye."

It has been remarked upon by several people, including his son Borys, that however emotional Conrad might become over trifles he had 'complete composure and competence when confronted with a real emergency.'

Early in 1890, Conrad received a boost to his morale. The *Academy* 'crowned' his *Tales of Unrest* (1898), selecting one of the stories in the collection, *Karain*, for special praise and awarding Conrad 50 guineas.

In terms of his art, the years at Pent Farm were the most fruitful for Conrad.

Conrad exhausted himself over the 'intense creative effort' required for the writing of *Nostromo*, a novel which must have been initially inspired by Cunninghame Graham and his knowledge of South America. Unfortunately, in spite of his intense effort, *Nostromo* (1904) did not receive the critical acclaim Conrad had hoped for. It was, he said, with the public 'the blackest possible frost.' His health began to deteriorate during the writing of this novel, and then, in 1904, Jessie injured her knees in a fall and was to remain a semi-cripple for the rest of her life. Matters did not improve with the Conrads. Conrad's bankers, Watson & Co., failed. To his friend Krieger, Conrad wrote: 'I've no banker after Watson's failure.'

They went to Capri where Conrad hoped to rest and to write, but it was to be one of their typically disastrous trips. The nurse looking after Jessie became ill, Conrad suffered from influenza, bronchitis, insomnia and nerves, and could not tolerate the climate, and he was again short of money. It was fortunate that, in the same year, through the influence of friends, he was given a grant of £500 with the King's consent from a confidential official fund.

On his return to England, he was involved in the production of his one-act play, *One Day More*: 'I don't think I am a dramatist,' he concluded, and he later wrote: 'I have a secret horror of all actors and actresses.'

During the year 1905 to 1906, Conrad was working on The Mirror of the Sea (a recollection of his experiences as a sailor), on the novel called *Chance*, on several short stories, including An Anarchist and *The Informer*—later published in a collection of six stories *A Set of Six*—and on *The Secret Agent* which he finished in 1906. For the three latter works he turned to the sensational subject of the anarchy, no doubt in part through Ford's connections with anarchists.

On August 1906, his second son, John, was born at the Galsworthy's London house in Addison Road, and after finishing *The Secret Agent* in November Conrad, 'feeling seedy and horribly depressed,' took his family off to the Continent again, to Montpellier and Geneva. The trip was bad again.

They returned home in the summer of 1907. 'No more trips abroad', Conrad wrote. He stayed in England for the next seven years, but not in the same house. He decided he could not longer live at Pent Farm, and in September 1907 the Conrads moved house again. They were to move three times between 1907 and 1910, to Sometiries in Bedfordshire for over a year, to Aldington in Kent, and in 1910 to Capel House, an isolated farmhouse near Ashford.

In 1908 Conrad was fifty. As an author he had had great acclaim, but *Nostormo* and *The Secret Agent* had been disappointments, and he was oppressed by the fact that he was not 'selling' author. He was tormented by the need to make money and the need to retain his artistic integrity.

Conrad had himself made a bid for a popularity in choosing a sensational subject for *The Secret Agent*, but he was a difficult novelist whose complex methods of narration and use of broken time sequences militated against popularity.

In 1902, William Blackwood had told Conrad that he was a loss to the firm–this after the sales of *Lord Jim*!–and it led Conrad to defend his artistic intention. 'I must not by any means be taken for a gifted loafer intent on living upon credulous publishers.' Criticism of his 'method' only irritated him. To Glasworthy, who suggested that the play adapted form *The Secret Agent* might be cut, he retorted: 'Indeed I have often felt that not only Third but the Second Act could come out altogether. After all: why the Professor? Why the Assistant Commissioner? Even Inspector Heat himself would be sufficiently characterized by his appearance in Third Act...what is that old woman [Winne Verloc's mother] doing there? She too could be eliminated: and also Mr. Valdimir.' And taking up critic's charge that his novel *Chance* could have been cut to half its present size, Conrad answered: 'No doubt that by selecting a certain method and taking great pains the whole story might have been written out on a cigarette paper.'

Under severe mental stress arising from these difficulties, and suffering form malarial gout, Conrad was nevertheless writing *Under Western Eyes* and "The Secret Sharer" collaborating on The Nature of a Crime with Ford, and composing his autobiographical *A Personal Record* for the *English Review* which Ford was now editing. In 1909 he quarrelled with Ford over this—'His conduct is *impossible*...He is a megalomaniac who imagines that he is managing the universe'—and they were never really reconciled.

Perhaps, given Conrad's highly strung, pessimistic nature, and his deep absorption in his work, a breakdown would have been, under any circumstances, inevitable. His work exhausted him because he so completely immersed himself in his fictional world. Conrad's pessimism as to mankind's condition was complete, and its influence in his work was not conducive to popularity: 'What makes mankind tragic is not that they are the victims of nature, it is that they are conscious of it. But as soon as you know of your slavery the pain, the anger, the strife–the tragedy begins.' He graphically explained his view of the universe in a letter to Cunninghame Graham: "There is a– let us say– machine. It evolved itself...out of a chaos of scraps of iron and behold!–it knits. I am horrified at the horrible work and stand appalled. I feel it ought to embroider– but it goes on knitting...You cannot by any special lubrication make embroidery with a knitting machine. And the most withering thought is that the infamous thing has made itself; made itself without thought, without conscience, without foresight, without eyes, without heart...It knits us in and it knits us out. It has knitted time, space, pain, death, corruption, despair and the illusions—and nothing matters. I'll admit however that to look at the remorseless process is sometimes amusing."

It is not surprising that Bertrand Russell (who met him first in 1913) said of him, 'I felt...that he though of civilized and morally tolerable human life as a dangerous walk on a thin crust of barely cooled lava which at any moment might break and let the unwary sink into fiery depths.'

But his fortune was about to change. In 1911 he was given a Civil List Pension of £ 100, and in the following year an American lawyer, Jon Quinn, wrote offering to buy his manuscripts. But more important, he was then working on *Chance* (1913) he had started six years earlier and which was to be his first best-seller. Conrad was unashamedly seeking popularity, and rewrote the end of the novel to make it 'nicer.' Garnett held the view that 'it is probable that the figure of the lady on the 'jacket.' of *Chance* did more to bring the novel into favour than a long review by Sir Sidney Colvin in *The Observer*.' But it was Sir Hugh Clifford who persuaded the proprietor of the *New York Herald* to take an interest in Conrad's work, and it was here that *Chance* was serialized. This had the effect of making a young man called Alfreed Knopf, who worked for the publishers Doubleday, persuade his employers to put the full weight of promotion behind Conrad's book. It was a best-seller on both sides of the Atlantic.

At this time Conrad met Richard Curie, a young man with whom he was to form a lasting friendship and who was to write many books about him.

In May of 1912, Conrad, having finished *Chance*, began a short story which ultimately grew into a novel *Victory* (1914). Conrad's hero here is Axel Heyst, an extraordinarily reticent man living in the tropics, whose philosophical father had instilled in him one command in face of a distrust of mankind: 'Look on-make no sound.' Pinker, thanks to the immense success of *Chance*, was able to sell the serial rights of *Victory* for £ 1,000 and on the strength of his new financial success, Conrad planned a trip to Poland.

The First World War had begun. The Conrads took refuge with a relative who had a house in the Carpathians, but in early October Conrad decided they must try to get home. They stayed in Vienna five days, since Conrad had gout. From Milan he cabled Pinker for money. They reached England on 3 November. Jessie commented, 'We had a narrow escape.'

Borys Conrad joined the army.

Conrad produced little during the war, though he did write The Shadow-Line in 1915. In 1917, although he published little he had in income of £ 2,000.

After this, he was interested in the dramatization of *Victory* being carried out by Macdonald Hastings, and begun to write *The Arrow of Gold*. *The Arrow of Gold* (1919) deals in part with Conrad's own experience in Marseilles. In 1919 he succeeded in finishing *the Rescue,* the novel he began on his honeymoon twenty-three years earlier. In October they moved to Oswalds, a Georgian house at Bishopsbourne, near Canterbury, which was to be Conrad's last home. Jessie was having more trouble with her knee and had another operation. They were comparatively wealthy—film rights for his books brought in about £4,000. Yet Conrad was still difficulties and he considered living partly in France to escape heavy taxation. In 1920 he begun what was to be his last work *Suspense,* a Napoleonic novel, and in January 1921, went with Jessie to Corsica, staying in Ajaccio, where he did some background reading for the novel. But Corsica was 'Cold. Wet, Horrors.' In December, he was writing a short story which grew to be his last completed novel, *The Rover* (1923).

He was now one of the most famous living authors in Britain and the United States and in 1923 made his only visit to America. He sailed to New York in the *Tuscania,* Captain Bone commanding. He was welcomed in America. He refused to lecture, but gave a talk at the house of fashionable hostess, Mrs. Curtiss James. 'I began at 9.45 and ended exactly at 11. There was a most attentive silence, some laughs and at the end, when I read the chapter of Lena's death, audible snuffling...It was a great experience.'

But he was greeted on his return home with the news of Borys' secret marriage. His response was, 'I don't want to know anything more about it.' However, Borys Conrad recalls that 'Characteristically, he uttered no reproaches when we met...' In November 1923, John Quinn sold his collection of Conrad manuscripts which he had been collecting for many years. He had bought them when Conrad was little read, but he was now a renowned author, and Conrad reckoned that Quinn made 1,000 per cent profit. The manuscript of *Victory* brought $ 8,000. Conrad said sadly that 'he hadn't got his share of the plunder.' Now Conrad was quite sick. In May Ramsay MacDonald sent him an envelope offering him the Knighthood. Conrad did not open it being alarmed that it was a letter from the department of income tax.'

In July he suffered a heart attack, and wrote to Earnest Dowson, 'I begin to feel like a cornered rat.' He said 'I am finished.' In the evening, Borya and John called on him. Jessie was in bed in the next room, only just back from the nursing home. 'Good night Boy,' he said to Borys. You know I am really ill this time.' Early next morning, he called to his wife, 'You Jess, I am better this morning. I can always get a rise out of you.' At eight-thirty he slid to the floor from his chair. He was dead. He was buried in Canterbury on 7 August 1924.

Conrad is one of the strangest figures in English literature—a Pole in English dress, first a sailor then earning a mighty reputation as a writer in a tongue not his own. He published his first novel in 1895, but did not have popular success until 1913—and thus could only be said to be known as a celebrity in England for a decade before he died. Moreover, he remained a mysterious figure all his life, who had lived in many of the obscure corners of the earth, and who was himself, a supreme example of a touching destiny.

2 Joseph Conard's Novels

Joseph Conrad is an entirely different and difficult writer of the 20th century English literature. This is because of the reason that he comes from a different and difficult background. He was a Pole, captain and from non-literary background. The concepts of 'Pole,' 'captain' and 'non-literary' backgrounds make much difference when one studies him in the circle of modernist English writers. The present chapter examines his fiction. As a matter of fact, Conrad's popular/major novels are *Almayer's Folly* (1895), *The Nigger of the 'Narcissus'* (1897), *Heart of Darkness* (1902), *Lord Jim* (1900), *Typhoon* (1903), *Nostromo* (1904), *Under the Western Eyes* (1911), *Chance* (1913) and *Victory* (1915). On the other hand, his novels such as *An Outcast of the Islands* (1896), *The Secret Agent* (1907), *Freya of the Seven Isles* (1902), *The Shadow Line* (1917), *The Arrow of Gold* (1919), *The Rescue* (1920), *The Rover* (1923), *Suspense* (1925) and *The Sisters* (1928) are much weak and unpopular. Some of them, like *Suspense* and *The Sisters,* are incomplete. The following is a critical analysis of this.

Almayer's Folly (1895)

Almayer is based on Charles Olmeijer whom Conrad met in Bornio in 1888. The author anglicized the hero's name. Olmeijer worked as a representative of Captain William Lingard (Tom Lingard in the novel). The historical Olmeijer had three friends (against one of Almayer) and four children (against one, Nina to Almayer). Conrad began the novel in idleness and wrote it for five years. The novel appeared by Fischer Unwin in 1895. The novel was received warmly as if a literary surprise.

Arthur Waugh noted in the *Critic* that Borneo, 'a tract hitherto untouched by the novelist,' was now 'annexed by Mr. Joseph Conrad, a new writer'; the *Spectator* critic hoped that Conrad might become 'the Kipling of the Malay Archipelago' (a remark that incidentally draws attention to Conrad's late start as a writer, since he was eight years older than Kipling); and the *Saturday Review* critic H. G. Wells, ventured to predict that the novel would secure its author 'a high place among contemporary story-tellers.' Norman Page observes, "*Almayer's Folly* is written in an assurance found in few first novels. Even more surprisingly it is written in an English style that is for the most part free from lapses, in idiom, and indeed, in many passages, remarkably expressive." As far as literary models are concerned, however, Conrad's first novel has affinities with more than one genre of fiction popular at the time. It is at once a love story, a novel of adventure, and an exercise in exoticism; and readers of the period would have been acquainted with this kind of fictional mixture in the work of such successful authors as R. L. Stevenson and H. Rider Haggard. But, as Ian Watt persuasively argues, Conrad seems to follow, but actually undermines, the prescriptions of popular romance.

In his sense of isolation and of being imprisoned by circumstances, Almayer anticipates many later Conradian protagonists. The narrator comments in Chapter 7 that "the sense of his absolute loneliness came home to his heart with a force that made him shudder" and two chapters later, when the Dutch lieutenant threatens to arrest him Almayer himself exclaims "Arrest! Why, I have been trying to get out of this infernal place for twenty years, and I can't, and adds a little later, 'You think there is one dead man here? Mistake, I assure you I am much more dead." Almost from the first, we realize that his dreams of wealth and retirement to the Europe he never seen is doomed to disappointment.

Ian Watt notes the Darwinian element in the novel, a respect in which it anticipates *Heart of Darkness* as well as the implications of biological determinism in the treatment of Almayer's wife and daughter. H.G. Wells identified the central conception of the novel as 'the relapse.... From the colonial version of civilization to a barbaric life,' another anticipation of *Heart of Darkness*. Fredrick Karl has pointed out that Conrad's first novel represents, structurally and technically, a break with nineteenth century traditions of English fiction. *Almayer's Folly* similar in structure to the Flaubertian novel in which unity of plot predominates, is a radical departure from the multiple plots of the Victorians, and, along with *The River* is perhaps the simplest of Conrad's novels.

F.A. Inamadar observes, "The river in *Almayer's Folly* is pivotal, and constitutes the central symbol, its mood and vagaries reflect Almayer's thoughts. He has on it such great trust that his life and death depend upon its favours and frowns. It controls the entire action of *Almayer's Folly* on all its levels." Conrad himself said that the novel is "A Story of the Eastern River," a fact that has been grasped by the critics as well. "The River being the usual medium for the appearance of the others," wrote Charles J. McCann, "is the unifying image of the book." Mr. Vink in the novel says in an explanatory whisper: "You know he (Lingard) has discovered a river."

An Outcast of the Islands (1896)

An Outcast of the Islands is Jeseph Conrad's second, and of course, less popular novel. This follows the theme and pattern of his first novel *Almayer's Folly*. *An Outcast of the Islands* has similar colonial or diasporic theme, where a European is joined to a native woman in the jungle. Willems' career in *An Outcast of the Islands* is similar to that of Almayer in *Almayer's Folly*. Both men are initially clerks working humbly for Huding in Macassar while desiring better things for themselves. They are further alike, and distinct from most of Conrad's later heroes in that their ideal consists chiefly in personal advancement and gain. In pursuit of their respective personal goals both men advance by contracting interracial marriages with the daughters of wealthy capitalists; Almayer takes the adopted Malay protégée of Lingard, while Willems marries the half-caste Joanna who turns out to be the natural child of old Hudig. In each case the marriage begins a train of events which leads to the hero's isolation in Sambir, a black world which contrasts as an inverted mirror image with the white world of his origin. Both men then continue their strivings in a hostile jungle context to the point where the tensions they create bring about their deaths. Both men, in their closing stages project their ideals on to a female, Almayer's Nina and Willems Aissa, who is in each case a native of the Malay world; and in each case there is both an anti-heroine opposing the native woman's association with the hero and a male rival for the heroine's affections.

An Outcast of the Island exhibits immediately the constant features of the Conradian pattern, a hero who in striving towards a goal, makes a dubious, compromising move and finds himself caught as a result in a dualistic universe where his every significant action is countered or frustrated. Willems's ideal, very like Almayer's is self-agradisement, in pursuit of which he embarks upon a career which receives its first real impulse when, at Hudig's behest, he marries Joanna, a half-caste woman who is later revealed to be his employer's daughter. This move is very close to the compromise made by Almayer in agreeing to wed Lingard's adopted daughter. Both men take women to whom they are personally indifferent in return for the patronage and promises for a powerful, wealthy father-in-law, and in each case the marriage of convenience involves the compromise that the woman is of a race regarded as inferior by the local whites. The marriages, emblematic of paradox, announce Conrad's major theme, the inherent self-frustration of human endeavour, for in each case the hero, in pursuit of social elevation, contracts a marriage which, although profitable, is felt to be socially degrading.

Willems marries Hudig's daughter. The woman is rich, but her relations are poor. Willems himself is a lazy fellow. He wants short cuts for success.

Willems failure as a seaman is symptomatic of this laxity. Conrad says, "The boy (young Willems) was hopelessly at variance with the spirit of the sea. He had an instinctive contempt for the honest simplicity of that work which led to nothing he cared for" (p. 17). The same desire for an "easy berth," clearly recognizable in Wait, Jim, Verloc, and the young hero of *The Shadow-Line,* causes Willems to fall into the arranged marriage with Hudig's daughter and later leads him to embezzlement as an alternative to self-discipline.

Willems' attempt to achieve wealthy respectability in Macassar lands him ironically in Sambir and activates the mechanism of a dualistic situation by which he is eventually destroyed. The antithesis of black and white worlds the jungle of Sambir and the gardens of Macassar works in much the same way here in *Almayer's Folly.*

S.K. Land writes, "Willems's situation in Macassar, in which he attaches himself to a woman, steals from her father, and is eventually confronted with his crime, is closely repeated in Sambir, where he steals Aissa from Omar, betrays Lingard's secrets in order to keep her, and is marooned in punishment by Lingard on his return. Moreover Willem's movement in Sambir, principally his usurpation of Lingard's authority and association with Assia, are countered from the white world by the association with Assia, by the successive arrivals of Lingard and Joanna. The dynamism of the plot consists essentially in the tension created by the antithetical tendencies of these two worlds, a situation first precipitated by the hero's strivings and only resolved by his death."

In Sambir, where Willems re-enacts a black version of his Macassar life, this same ability and lack of scruple enables him to become temporarily a leader and arbiter of local destiny. The hero of Conrad's second novel is more complex than *Almayer* in being not only flawed but also exceptional, and the mirror-world of Sambir reflects not only his failure but also his achievement. Williams, as the man of great promise who turns out to be unsound, prefigures the line of more developed paradoxical heroes which begins with Wait and Kurtz.

Willems in Sabmir is therefore not simply an outcast but also, as Assia calls him, "the great man of the place" (p. 70). It is this aura of unspecified greatness that attracts Assia to him. Conrad writes, "To her he was something new, unknown and strange. He was bigger, stronger than any man she had seen before, and altogether different from all those she knew. He was of the victorious race. With a vivid remembrance of the great catastrophe of her life he appeared to her with all the fascination of a great and dangerous thing; of a terror vanquished, surmounted made a plaything of. They spoke with just such a deep voice those victorious men; they looked with just such hard blue eyes at their enemies. And she made that voice speak softly to her, those eyes look tenderly at her face. He was indeed a man" (p. 75).

Assia is the symbol of Willems's success and the embodiment of his ideal in the black world, just as is Joanna in the white. Joanna emerges from the cultivated gardens and social milieu of Macassar, much as Assia is identified with the jungle background in which Willems finds her, the "very spirit of that land of mysterious forests" (p. 70). Each woman comes to Willems finally as reward for the exercise of his commercial acumen, in helping first Hudig and then Abdulla to promote their trades, the same sharp practice which also in each world respectively, involves him in theft and betrayal.

Both Joanna and Aissa are first attracted to Willems by his reputed greatness, and each woman becomes in turn the auditor of his self glorifying monologues. Joanna in Macassar was made to get up at nights when Willems came home late and to listen to him "explaining ... how great and good he was" (p. 9); in Sambir Willems tells Aissa the story of his life, which "she made up for herself into a story of a man great amongst his own people" (p. 75). Each woman in turn, as receptor of Willems's view of himself and as his reward for practical achievement, signifies his goal in life, one in the white world, the other in the black. The structure of the story, with the Sambir episode at its centre, confirms Aissa as the heroine in terms of our pattern. Joanna, drab figure of passionless conventionality and Willems' lawful wife, is a typical anti-heroine, returning at the end of the story to preside over the hero's final divorce from Aissa. Joanna's object at that late stage is to fetch Willems back to the world he has deserted, the world of their marriage, his business connections, and white respectability.

His relationship with the heroine, symptomatic of Willems over all position in Sambir, is ambiguous and ultimately unsatisfactory. He is himself a man of paradox, a man of exceptional cleverness yet with weaknesses which render him stupid and, like the typical Conradian hero, he is caught in a paradoxical situation between two words.

As Willems falls increasingly under Aissa's spell he senses a gradual "flight of (his) old self" (p. 69), a loss of "individuality" (p. 77). "He seemed to be surrendering to a wild creature the unstained purity of his life, of his trace, of his civilization. He had a notion of being lost among shapeless things that were dangerous and ghastly" (p. 80). Just as Willems's deeper sexual instincts, of which he seems scarcely aware, make him dissatisfied with Joanna, so, conversely, his sense of the white world's civilized proprieties makes him ashamed of and resistant to his desire for Aissa. "He feels contempt for himself as the slave of a passion he had always derided, as the man unable to assert his will. This will, all his sensations, his personality—all this seemed to be lost in the abominable desire, in the priceless promise of that woman" (pp. 128-9).

Omar is in line with most of the later Conradian rivals: Cornelius in *Lord Jim*, Schomberg in *Victory*, Ortega in *The Arrow of Gold*, Mr Travers in *The Rescue*, and Scevola in *The Rover*.

The rival's role is typically a small one, but may none the less be a factor in bringing the catastrophe upon the hero, usually as a result of an attempted act of jealous vengeance after the hero's intervention has carried off the heroine. Omar is aroused by what is, from his point of view, Willems's "theft" of Aissa. Almayer points this out, indicating at the same time the parallelism between this theft and Willems's *appropriation of Hudig's funds* in Macassar. "So you did steal,' he went on, with repressed exultation. "I thought there was something of the kind. And now, here, you steal again .... Oh, I don't' mean from me. I haven't missed anything.... But that girl. Hey! You stole her. You did not pay the old fellow. She is no good to him now, is she?" (p. 89). Omar, the "old fellow," who is blind and on the verge of death, therefore makes apathetic attempt to kill Willems, which is easily prevented by Aissa but which shows Willems for the first time the underlying falsity of his position in Sambir.

Lingard is recognizable as a nemesis figure in *An Outcast of the Islands* when his part there is compared to the line of similar roles in the later novels. There is no very clear *alter ego* relationship between Lingard and Willems, but Lingard does meet the criteria of coming into the story after the hero has committed an act of betrayal.

Willems is the first of a line of Conradian heroes who attempt to achieve their ideal by committing some real or reputed offence, usually in the nature of a crime, against the world or code they are abandoning. Lingard is the first of the counteractive figures who are generally responsible for ending the heroes' careers.

S.K. Land says,"*An Outcast of the Islands* is in many ways a transitional work, itself a rather poorly structured piece, standing chronologically between the highly-crafted but much simpler *Almayer's Folly*, and the first product of Conrad's literary maturity, the superb *Nigger of the 'Narcissus.'*"

The Nigger of 'Narcissus' (1897)

This novel is a fine sea novel. Narrated by an anonymous seaman, the action concentrates on the human community of the ship, the

Narcissus, on its way from Bombay to London. The tensions within that small number are as perilous as the weather itself and are produced partly by two different generations of seamen. Captain Alistoun and the veteran Singleton have the reticence of men primarily concerned with their duties as seamen. Conversely, the detachment from the working community of the younger Donkin and of Wait, the Negro of the book's title, comes to represent a powerful, if less practical, set of interests.

The illness and confinement of Wait claim the humanitarian sympathies of the remaining crew. At the height of a storm five men chance their lives to save the trapped Wait from his deck cabin; as Singleton and Alistoun are uneasily aware, the safety of the entire ship is meanwhile at risk. Confrontation between the captain and Donkin (who supports Wait's demands to go back on duty) comes to a head. After Donkin has hurled a belaying pin in his direction, the captain calmly reasserts an authority, with the remaining crew looking on. More strangely, Singleton's superstition that Wait will die at the first sight of land comes true.

In *The Nigger of the 'Narcissus'* Conrad identifies truth with one side of his dualistic universe. The dialectical structure remains unchanged and the hero is still obliged to die, caught between the conflict of forces. His initial act has unleashed; but in this story the values are shifted as one party vindicated in the cosmic struggle and allowed to bring his ship world intact to a safe harbour. Wait dies, releasing the *Narcissus* to bear her reclaimed crew under their victorious Captain to a good pay-day. With the partial exceptions of *Chance* and *The Rover*, all of Conrad's other longer works have more or less Wagnerian endings, in which either the hero is defeated or the endless cyclical struggle between the two sides is emphasized. *The Nigger of 'Narcissus'* is unique in its positive conclusion, for which the reason is again Allistoun.

The Nigger of the 'Narcissus' is the first of the books to carry deliberately and with care the burden of several major interests and various minor ones. The one interest which existed for most readers in 1897 remains a real one today; the faithful document of life and adventure at sea. The story is indeed the tribute to the "Children of the sea" that Conrad wanted it to be: a memorial to a masculine society and the successful seizing of a passing phase of life from the remorseless rush of time. It is certainly a tribute to this particular ship on which Conrad chose to sail in 1884. But it is also a study in collective psychology; and also, frankly, a symbolic comment on man's nature and destiny; and also, less openly, a prose poem carrying overtones of myth.

The pattern followed in the first novel *Almayer's Folly* (1895) is repeated in this third novel. In the first novel there words, Almayer, Folly and River are linked and likewise the words, Nigger, the 'Narcissus' and the Sea are linked here. F. A. Inamdar observes, "*Almayer's Folly* is the tale of the river. A peculiar moral dilemma appears in Almayer and Willems as a result of betrayal; Almayer of his race, Willems's of his benefactor, Lingard. The same theme of betrayal, this time by a group rather than by an individual, is expressed in the third novel as in the first two, through colour symbolism. The same pattern of abyss and fall recurs in *The Nigger of the 'Narcissus.'* As Almayer foolishly strives to be pure in a chaotic wilderness of darkness and decay, so the crew in the third novel seek gentility but steadily become mutineers and decay, because they refuse to acknowledge the blackness of their hearts, they insist blindly on their rights as honourable men. After they identify themselves with the Nigger, they become inhabitants of a Waste Land. Their pilgrimage too ends in chaos and meaninglessness. Their descent from the human to the subhuman is similar to that of Almayer and Willems. Such a descent is worked out through the ship symbolism, light and dark and colour symbolism, and the stellar and meteorological imagery. The sea symbol is a background symbol on which the drama of their moral descent is enacted. As in the first novel, the characters themselves become symbols. For example, James Wait, and Donkin symbolize total evil; the passive evil represented by James Wait and the active evil symbolized by Donkin. Evil as negation is worked out through these principal characters. The crew itself become a symbol of fallen humanity. Captain Allistoun, Mr. Baker, the chief mate, and others symbolize God and His associates. The novel taken as a whole, is Conrad's version of *Paradise Lost.*"

Heart of Darkness (1902)

Joseph Conrad's novel *Heart of Darkness* is a narrative by Charlie Marlow, an officer in the Merchant's Navy who appears in Conrad's other works like *Lord Jim, Youth* and *Chance*. Sitting on board a ship anchored in the lower reaches of the River Thames, he tells a group of friends the story of his journey up the Congo River in Africa, in the employment of a Belgian trading company. Marlow is in the company of four people: the Director of the Company as the captain who resembled a pilot and a lawyer, 'the best of old fellows.' One of the other is an accountant. Marlow sat with them cross-legged.

Conrad says, "He had sunken cheeks, a yellow complexion, a straight back, an ascetic aspect, and, with his arms dropped, the palms of hands outwards, resembled an idol." All these sea-voyagers sat in a vessel called *Nellie,* a cruising yawl.

The ship left the Thames towards Gravesend in Kent via Deptford and Erith. The day was ending in a serenity of still and exquisite brilliance. The water of the river shone pacifically. Conrad speaks the river Thames served great seafarers like Francis Drake and Sir John Franklin. He speaks of the sea as a mysterious place. It is seamen's country; the ships in it being much the same in look. And the sea is the same everywhere.

Conrad says, "In the immutability of their surroundings the foreign shores, the foreign faces, the changing immensity of life, glide past, veiled not by a sense of mystery to a slightly disdainful ignorance; for there is nothing mysterious to a seaman unless it be the sea itself, which is the mistress of his existence and as inscrutable as destiny"(p. 5).

> Marlow seemed like one —a perpetual wanderer. He says the seamen would suffer badly as they would have no worldly comforts ('No Falemian wine here, no going ashore'). Only their competence or 'efficiency' would save them. He went to such an interior of Congo in the wild of Africa. He says, "It was the farthest point of navigation and the culminating point of my experience. It seemed somehow to throw a kind of light on everything about me—and into my thoughts" (p. 7). He adds his going there was his boyhood dream. In fact, this was Conrad's dream as well. Such Congo for the author as well as for his hero was: "a place of darkness." But there was in it one river especially, almightily big river, that you could see on the map, resembling an immense snake uncoiled, with its head in the sea, its body at rest curving afar a vast country, and its tail lost in the depths of the land. So his aunt helped Marlow find

> out an assignment with the Belgian sea company. Marlow says his predecessor, a Dane, had died in his fighting with a black man over the small issue of two hens. When he entered the office of his job he met a white man. He glorified the company's success. There were two women maybe servants. When he visited a few places in the Congo he found the nature fascinating. But depressing blacks depressed him.: 'It was like a weary pilgrimage amongst hints for neighbours"(p. 14).

Marlow, in a French steamer, travels with a Swede, and reaches some destination. The description of the same is vivid: "At last we opened. A rocky cliff appeared, mounds of turned-up earth by the shore, houses on a hill, others with iron roofs, amongst a waste of excavations, or hanging to the declivity. A continuous noise of the rapids above hovered over this scene of inhabited devastation. A lot of people, mostly black and naked, moved about like ants. A jetty projected into the river. A blinding sunlight drowned all this at times in a sudden recrudescence of glare. 'There's your company's station,' said the Swede, pointing to three wooden barrack-like structures on the rocky slope"(p. 16). There Marlow finds lots of people—all suffering in a way or another. They were working in a barbarous manner maybe compelled by some tyrannical agents. It was a 'gloomy circle of some inferno.' There, "Black shapes crouched, lay, sat between the trees, leaning against the trunks, clinging to the earth, half coming out, half effaced within the dim light, in all the attitudes of pain, abandonment, and despair. An ther mine on the cliff went off, followed by a slight shudder of the soil under my feet. The work was going on. The work! And this was the place where some of the helpers had withdrawn to die"(p. 17). Conrad remarks the blacks were dying slowly. Then Marlow goes to the company station where he finds a white man, an accountant. He lives there for two days—'an eternity.' This accountant, his speech and information about Kurtz are explicit below:

"One day he remarked, without lifting his head, 'In the interior you will no doubt meet Mr Kurtz. On my asking who Mr Kurtz was, he said he was a first class agent; and seeing my disappointment at this remarkable person.' Further questions elicited from him that Mr Kurtz was at present in charge of a trading post, a very important one, in the true ivory-country, at 'the very bottom of there. Sends in as much ivory as all the others put together....' He began to write again. "The sick man was too ill to groan. The flies buzzed in a great peace"(p. 19). "So the next day Marlow leaves with a caravan of sixty men for a two hundred mile tramp. The path was very bad and paths and paths everywhere.... Abandoned villages.... A great silence around and above.... After 20 miles of travel Marlow and his crew reach an inner station and meet its master. He says, 'My first interview with the manager was curious. He did not ask me to sit down after my twenty-mile walk that morning. He was commonplace in complexion, in feature, in manners, and in voice. He was of middle size and of ordinary build' (p. 22). "As Marlow says the man's asset was neither his genius nor his efficiency, but average work-ethic. He was a common trader. He did not originate anything. He spoke to Marlow about Kurtz's difficulty and his station being in danger. He says Kurtz was the best agent, an exceptional man, of the greatest importance to the company. Marlow detests his lying. He detested it as a taint of death. Marlow comes across an Eldorado Exploring Expedition, which was carrying its loot in the land of loot and lawlessness.

In the part II of the novel Conrad depicts Marlow's sensibilities about Kurtz. We come to know that Kurtz is a half caste, born and brought up in England to his father—a half-Englishman and mother a half-French woman. It is said he was created in Europe. Continuing his expedition Marlow comes nearer Kurtz's station. He is all eager to meet him who is the hero of Congo's ivory trade. Marlow notices cannibalists on the way. His way is full of wild—trees, trees, millions of trees. The mystery of the forest is there. Marlow says, "We were cut off from the comprehension of our surroundings; we glided past like phantoms, wondering and secretly appalled, as sane men would be before an enthusiastic outbreak in a madhouse. We could not understand because we were too far and could not remember, because we were traveling in the night of first ages, of those ages that are gone, leaving hardly a sign—and no memories"(p. 38).

Conrad's narration of Marlow's adventure for visiting Kurtz runs complex. It is full of suspense and thrill. The writer says, "Some fifty miles below the Inner Station we (Marlow and his pilgrims (juts people) came upon a hut of reeds, an inclined and melancholy pole, with the unrecognizable tatters of what had been a flag of some sort flying from it, and a neatly stacked wood-pole. This was unexpected" (p. 38). There is a reference to life's misery and suffering. Marlow tells his companion that: "I observed with assumed innocence that no man was safe from trouble in this world"(p. 39). There was thick fog. Finally Marlow meets Kurtz and the latter is about to die because of some disaster. There is not much conversation between the two. Meanwhile attributed to some calamity or danger, Marlow hears the news of Kurtz's fall. In his words: "And by the way, I suppose Mr. Kurtz is dead as well by this time"(p. 47).

Kurtz was known for his ivory business. He used to collect it in heaps. His old mud shanty was bursting with it. "You would think there was not a single tusk left either above or below the ground in the whole country"(p.49). Kurtz had taken a high seat amongst the devils of the land. Marlow learns that Kurtz was also in charge of some humanitarian aid. The International Society for the Suppression of Savage Customs had entrusted him with the making of a report for its future guidance. And he had written it too. "He began with the argument that we whites, from the point of development we had arrived at, 'must necessarily appear to them (savages) in the nature of supernatural beings—we approach them with the might as of a deity, and so on. By the simple exercise of our will we can exert a power for good practically unbounded etc"(p. 51). On the other hand, the whites had in their agenda the act of exterminating the brutes. So Marlow hears much about Kurtz's death and the burning of his station. Marlow meets another white civilized man—a Russian—on the way. He was a close acquaintance of Kurtz. He tells he worked with Kurtz. This man looks like an insoluble problem. The man says Kurtz was a genius. He discovered several villages, a lake too. His expeditions were mainly for ivory.

"He came to them (the Negroes) with thunder and lightening, you know—and they had never seen anything like it—and very terrible. He could be very terrible. You can't judge Mr Kurtz as you would an ordinary man. No, no, no! Now—just to give you an idea—I don't mind telling you, he wanted to shoot me too one day—but I don't judge him.' Shoot you!' I cried. 'What for?' 'Well, I had a small lot of ivory the chief of that village near my house gave me, and wouldn't hear reason. He declared he would shoot me unless he could do so, and had a fancy for it, and there was nothing on earth to prevent him killing whom he jolly well pleased. And it was true too. I gave him the ivory. What did I care! But I didn't clear out. No, no. I couldn't leave him. I had to be careful, of course, till we got friendly again for a time. He had his second illness then. Afterwards I had to keep out of the way; but I didn't mind. He was living for the most part in those villages on the lake. When he came down to the river, sometimes he would take to me, and sometimes it was better for me to be careful. This man suffered too much. He hated all this, and somehow he couldn't get away. When I had a chance I begged him to try and leave while there was time; I offered to go back with him. And he would say yes, and then he would remain; go off on another ivory hunt; disappear for weeks; forget himself amongst these people—forget himself—you know"(p. 57). Marlow hears that Kurtz lacked restraint in the gratification of his various lusts. There is a reference that he was hallow at the core ethically. Kurtz in German meant 'short.' It also came true in his life and death.

Marlow who, for times, takes Kurtz down the Inner Station thinks he is an immortal. Conrad says, "Kurtz discovered. A voice! A voice! It rang deep to the very last. It survived his strength to hide in the magnificent folds of eloquence the barren darkness of his heart. Oh, he struggled! He struggled! The waters of his weary brain were haunted by shadowy images now—images of wealth and fame revolving obsequiously round his inextinguishable gift of noble and lofty expression"(p. 69). It is said Kurtz's work was an impenetrable darkness. Marlow feels, "Kurtz was a remarkable man. He had something to say. He said it. Since I had peeped over the edge myself, I understood between the meaning of his stare that could not see the flame of the candle, but was wise enough to embrace the whole universe, piercing enough to penetrate all the hearts that beat in the darkness. He had summed up—he had judged. "The Horror!' He was a remarkable man"(p. 72). Once Kurtz passes away, there appear his possible friends and others. One of his cousins appears. He says Kurtz was a musician. It is heard that he was a painter-cum-journalist. That means he was a universal genius. Marlow writes, "This visitor informed me Kurtz's proper sphere ought to have been politics. Some say he should have been an extremist. Marlow finds some of Kurtz's letters and a portrait of a girl, maybe his African Mistress. Later it is said his mother passes away."

Marlow says he returned to Europe afterwards. There is a dialogue at the end of the novel relating to his conversation to Kurtz's fiancée in Europe. On hearing Kurtz's story she bursts forth:

"And of all this,' she went on mournfully, ' of all his promise and of all his greatness, of his generous mind, of his noble heart, nothing remains—nothing but a memory. You and I—'

"We shall always remember him,' said Marlow.

...

"To the very end,' I said shakily. 'I heard his very last words....'I stopped in a fright.

"'Repeat them,' she murmured in a heart-broken tone.' I want I want—something—something—to—to live with."

...

"'The last word he pronounced was—your name' "

(pp. 78-79).

Once the narration is over Marlow sits like a Buddha in all his quietitude, remembering the immensity of darkness.

As we know Conrad wrote *Heart of Darkness* in 1899. The same year it was serialized in the *Blackwood's Magazine* in three installments. The story evoked a mixed response. It was taken for an attack upon the Belgian expedition in the Congo. Some called it a moral tract; and as a study of race relationships. Robert F. Haugh observes, "*The Bookman* called it, "a symbolic picture of the inborn antagonisms of two races, the white and the black." *The Spectator,* without indicating that it understood the story any better, praised the moral tone. Most of the contemporary reviewers read it as a criticism of Belgian colonialism, an issue that remained alive until Conrad's death and got attention in his obituary notices." Edward Garnett who introduced Conrad in English society said it is "A most amusing consummate piece of artistic diablerie—an analysis of the white man's morale when let loose from European restraint and planted down in the tropics as an 'emissary of light' armed to the teeth to make trade profits out of subject races." E. M Forster remarked: "What is so elusive about him (Conrad) is that he is always promising to make some general philosophical statement about the universe, and then refraining in a gruff declaimer..... there is a central obscurity, something noble, heroic, inspiring half-a-globe great books, but obscure! Obscure!" F. R. Leavis said that Conrad's Kurtz was an appropriate source for the epigraph of *The Hollow Men*. Critics viewed the character of the hero very differently. Joseph Warren Beach said: "Kurtz is a personal embodiment, a dramatization, of all that Conrad felt of futility, degradation, and horror in what the Europeans in the Congo called 'progress,' which meant the exploitation of the natives by every variety of cruelty and treachery known to greedy man. Kurtz was to Marlow, penetrating this country, a name, constantly recurring in people's talk, for cleverness and enterprise.... The blackness and mystery of his character tone in with the savage mystery of the Congo, and they develop *pari passu* with the atmosphere of shadowy horror." This development is conducted cumulatively by insensitive degrees, by carefully correlated new items, new intimations; and all this process is controlled through the consciousness of Marlow. Thus we have a triumph of atmospheric effect produced with the technique of the limited point of view, a story in a class with "The Fall of the House of Usher" and "The Turn of the Screw." Beach calls Marlow as Kurtz's brother as identified in the climax of the story. Indeed, Marlow wanted to search the other in the darkness. Critics call Marlow as Kurtz's harlequin discipline.

In the view of H. L. Mencken, "Under all his stories there ebbs and flows a kind of tempered melancholy, a sense of seeking and not finding...." I take the words from a little book on Joseph Conrad by Wilson Follott privately printed. "They define both the mood of the stories as works of art and their burden and direction as criticisms of life....The conviction that human life is a seeking without a finding, that its purpose is impenetrable, that joy and sorrow are alike meaningless, you will see written largely in the work of most great creative artists." That means in Conrad's fiction, particularly *Heart of Darkness* that is his best, this sense of cosmic implacability or confession of unintelligibility is explicit. Mencken thinks the story of Kurtz is that it is pointless. Kurtz's death is as meaningless as his life, that the moral of such a sordid tragedy is a wholesale negation of all morals.

Conrad's novel is about a journey in the inner self of Marlow. Albert Guerard observes, "Conrad's *Heart of Darkness* begins with the friends on the yacht under the dark above Gravesend and at last returns to them, to the tranquil waterway that 'leading to the uttermost ends of the earth flowed somber under an overcast sky—seemed to lead into the heart of an immense darkness.'" A passage in the novel speaks of it as a primeval journey: "Going up the river was like traveling back to the earliest beginnings of the world, when vegetation rioted on the earth and the big trees were kings. An empty stream, a great silence, an impenetrable forest. The air was warm, thick, heavy, sluggish. There was no joy in the brilliance of sunshine. The long stretches of the waterway ran on, deserted, into the gloom of overshadowed distances. On silvery sandbanks hippos and alligators sunned themselves side by side."

The novel *Heart of Darkness* reads as a quest of the inner self. In fact, it has a scope for several interpretations. Jerome Thale comments: "Conrad's Heart of Darkness has all the trappings of the conventional adventure tale—mystery, exotic setting, escape, suspense, unexpected attack. These, of course, are only the vehicle of something more fundamental, and one way of getting at what they symbolize is to see the story as a great quest." Really Conrad's *Heart of Darkness* remains a great meditation in literature.

Lord Jim (1900)

"Any reading of *Lord Jim* that aspires to be comprehensive must come to terms with the novel's title-character. To borrow Emerson's words, he incarnates the 'plain old Adam, the simple genuine self against the whole world,' a notoriously unequal struggle with a foreordained outcome. Conrad's earlier Malay novels, the 'Lingard Trilogy' of *Almayer's Folly, An Outcast of the Islands,* and the unfinished 'The Rescuer,' similarly focus on individuals living in exile from their culture and blindly in pursuit of an unhappy fate."

However, it is not only about the sea that Cornad is a master storyteller but also about the people who go down to the sea in ships, and the torment of the soul occasioned by a moment's fall from honour. *Lord Jim,* based on a true story, recounts the story of Jim, the chief mate on the poorly-crewed *Patna*—a ship carrying pilgrims in Eastern seas—which threatens to sink and is abandoned by its officers who are joined by Jim at the last minute in all the confusion and chaos without conscious thought. The

Patna does not sink and the officers are rescued, but Jim alone faces the court of enquiry and, even wrose, the vivid torment of his own conscience at the breaking of a code of honour he holds dear.

The story continues with Jim's inability to escape from the shame of the incident on the *Patna,* despite the efforts of many well-disposed people to assist him. Eventually, Jim is sent to a remote trading station–Patusan–and there brings order and prosperity to a previously chaotic community, becoming in the process 'Tuan' or Lord Jim. A further incursion by disnonourable men into Jim's new world leads to his final confrontation with the issue of honour and final death.

Lord Jim was first published in serial form in *Blackwood's* Magazine 1899-1900. It was published as a book in 1900. Lord Jim was begun immediately after Conrad had finished writing "Youth" in the summer of 1898, dropped for a time, taken up again after he had written *Heart of Darkness,* and finished it in the summer of 1900. Conrad wrote, "But, seriously, the truth of the matter is, that my first thought was of a short story, concerned only with the pilgrim ship episode; nothing more. And that was a legitimate conception. After writing a few pages, however, I became for some reason discontented and I laid them aside for a time. I didn't take them out of the drawer till the late Mr. William Blackwood suggested I should give something again to his magazine."

In terms of plot there are undoubtedly two parts to the story: the defection of Jim and the disaster after he seems to have rehabilitated himself; certainly the second part has been added. But they are intimately connected. It is, indeed, difficult to imagine the first part alone as a satisfactory story—certainly as a story by Conrad; the account of cowardly leap for safety alone could hardly be enough; it demands development.

The ugly matter was this: "We shall be told that these officers had deserted their ship when it was facing a grave danger, and that they had completely disregarded the safety of the eight hundred pilgrims on board the ship. This was the naked and ugly fact. The ship had not perished as those officers had thought. The ship had reached the Aden port without any loss of life, barring one death. The important fact was that the officers had abandoned their ship at a time of danger, leaving the passengers to face the situation." (p. 64).

Jim's offence is one upon which the Court of Enquiry can have no mercy.

Finally, in the jungle settlement of Patusan, he rises to be "Lord Jim," one whose authority and honour are never questioned and on whom all the natives are dependent. It seems that he has successfully isolated himself from his past, in a place where the stream of civilization, as if divided on a headland, a hundred miles north of Patusan, branches east and south-west; leaving its plains and valleys, its old trees and its old mankind, neglected and isolated.

The reason for this uncertainty is clear; it is because Marlow, Conrad's mouthpiece, is himself bewildered. As in *Heart of Darkness*, which Conrad wrote while recasting the novel, Marlow plays a greater part than might at first be thought. We may reasonably wonder whether the feelings which brought *Heart of Darkness* to birth may not be the chief cause why *Lord Jim* developed from a simple short story into a complex novel, for there are many resemblances between the relationship of Marlow and Kurtz and that of Marlow and Jim.

It is obvious enough that Marlow is disturbed because Jim, a fellow English seaman, has not been true to the standards by which they all live. "I was aggrieved against him [he says], as though he had cheated me-me!—of a splendid opportunity to keep up the illusion of my beginnings, as though he had robbed our common life of the last spark of its glamour."

Marlow would seem here to be at one with Winnie Verloc of *The Secret Agent* in her belief that life does not bear looking into very closely, and he continues with the direct implication that such courage is only possible for fools. This has nothing to do with Jim, directly; only he was outwardly so typical of that good, stupid kind we like to feel marching right and left of us in life, of the kind that is not disturbed by the vagaries of intelligence and perversions of nerves.

The feeling of insecurity is deepened by the story of Brierly's suicide. That impeccable captain has felt the same apprehension as Marlow: "...the only thing that holds us together," he says, "is just the name for that kind of decency. Such an affair destroys one's confidence." We might feel the conclusion to be extreme, for in any group of men there will be some who will betray the faith reposed in them, but we know that, all the time he is enquiring into Jim's case, he is also sitting in judgment on himself and finding a verdict of unmitigated guilt. Marlow speculates that, in his case too, it is the awakening of some idea: "...the matter was no doubt of the gravest import one of those trifles that awaken ideas-start into life some thought with which a man unused to such a companionship finds it impossible to live. We are given no hint of what the idea is, except that it is not a commonplace worry about drink, or money, or women."

Widely considered a key work, even 'a supreme exemplar'of literary Modernism, *Lord Jim* unflinchingly challenges late nineteenth-century modes of perception and literary representation. Its final title–*Lord Jim, A Tale*–moves in contradictory directions, conflating the aristocratic with the intimate and the familiar, and the uniquely individual and 'real' with the collective and fictive.

One of the main fascinations and pleasures of *Lord Jim* resides in exploring the interrelationships between its array of narrative techniques—the use of a highly individualized frame narrator, chronological dislocations, impressionistic devices, ironic juxtapositions, thematic appositions, and delayed decoding, to name but the most obvious–and the intricate moral, philosophical, political, and ideological cruxes that these complex strategies introduce and elaborate.

J. H. Stape writes, "The characterization of the novel as the 'great poem of friendship in the Conrad canon' accurately captures the intensity Conrad brings to his exploration of this subject, embracing not only Marlow's affectionate concern for him but also Jim's cross-cultural and reciprocal friendship with Dain Waris as well as Marlow's friendship for Stein."

Typhoon (1902)

Gail Fraser thinks with *Typhoon*, written some two and half years later, Conrad continued to break new ground. Although a 'storm-piece' like *The Nigger of the /Narcissus'*, this story is concerned with the manifold ways in which the steamer's ordeal differs from that of a sailing ship. The division of crew members into 'sailors and firemen,' the patently unromantic labours of such as Hackett and Beale, the increased isolation of the captain—Conrad portrays these historical changes in a manner that combines *vivid* particulars with symbolic heightening.

Fraser observes, "This leap forward in time goes well beyond Maupassant's dictum that fiction presents an '*illusion* of reality' through 'selectivity' and 'orchestrated events.' A post-modernist in this respect at least, Conrad draws attention to the art of 'yarning' (associated with Jukes) and challenges the reader's imagination to fill the gap. The impact of the ellipsis is all the greater because to follow immediately upon a very different type of narrative chronology. In his graphic presentation of the storm and its twenty-minute period of calm, Conrad makes the time of the story and the time of the narrative as equal as possible. The result is to immerse readers in the 'real' ordeal and to emphasize the importance of 'direct' experience as a source of integrity and wisdom."

A reviewer in the *Manchester* Guardian said that 'Mr Conrad is now writing in the fulness of his power. *The Times Literary Supplement* reversed the kind of comparison between Conrad and Kipling, to Conrad's disadvantage, that had become commonplace, and declared that 'not even Kipling ... has quite the same power of intense vividness'. *The Morning Post* said that, as a writer of short stories, 'Mr Kipling is the only one who can be compared with him . . . if we allow Mr Kipling to be supreme on land, Mr Conrad has no equal on the seas.'

Typhoon was published in the *Pall Mall Magazine* in three instalments in 1922. It appears to have been written in 1900. In 1919 Conrad added an "Author's Note" in which he states that the central incident is based on real life but not on personal experience: he had heard it talked about in the East but had never met anybody personally concerned in this affair. The name of MacWhirr is borrowed from the captain under whom Conrad had served on the *Highland Forest*. The "Author's Note" also makes the important point that the real subject of the story is 'not the bad weather but the extraordinary complication brought into the ship's life at a moment of exceptional stress by the human element below her deck.'

Superficially, the story offers a powerful account of appalling weather conditions at sea, and on this level it works extremely well: the description of the force of the typhoon and its effect on the *Nan-Shan* is one of Conrad's finest pieces of descriptive writing. A notable feature of the narrative is his refusal to try to improve on or even to repeat, his own achievement: the second phase of the typhoon occurs in the space between the fifth and sixth chapters and goes entirely undescribed.

Beyond this, the story is a study of Captain MacWhirr, irresponsive and unruffled, having just enough imagination to carry him through each successive day and faithful to facts, which alone his consciousness reflected. Facts and imagina-tion are to turn out to be contrasting key-words of the story, and the dramatic and psychological heart of it is exposed in the final paragraph of the first chapter: "a man who had sailed over the surface of the oceans as some men go skimming over the years of existence to sink gently into a placid grave, ignorant of life to the last, without ever having been made to see all it may contain of perfidy, of violence, and of terror" is exposed to the immeasurable strength and the immoderate wrath of the passionate sea. At this point, and again later, we perceive that the simple narrative can also be read as a parable. Confronted with what he calls 'dirty weather', Mac Whirr's practical philosophy is not to try to evade it but to meet it head-on: as he tells Jukes, "A gale is a gale, . . . and a full-powered steamship has got to face it. There's just so much dirty weather blocking about the world, and the proper thing is to go through it...." At this point in the story his lack of imagination is a positive virtue. But even he is affected, and even his unpractised imagination is stirred, towards the end of chapter 5, when he puts a box of matches carefully back in its place and it occurs to him that perhaps he would never have occasion to use that box any more: the matchbox becomes the symbol of all these little habits that chain us to the weary round of life. He has been seriously discomposed, and has felt a sense of dismay reaching the very seat of his composure, by finding that the typhoon has intruded on his well-ordered arrangements - all the things that had their safe appointed places have been thrown around as if by some vandal. But a few lines later he reaches out for a towel and finds that that at least is in its appointed place. As Guerard aptly says, 'This humble moment is the story's climax. MacWhirr's next remark shows a return of dogged deter-mination: "She may come out of it yet."

The final chapter of this masterly tale shows that this crisis in MacWhirr's life has been completely misunderstood by those who know him best: his wife, reading a letter in which he tells her about the typhoon, totally fails to perceive the drama of his self-revelation; and the last words are the uncomprehending verdict of Jukes, "I think that he got out of it very well for such a stupid man."

Nostromo (1904)

In 1907, Conrad wrote to his literary agent, J. B. Pinker, that 'the public mind runs on questions of war and peace and labour.' He adds that he plans 'to treat those subjects...from a modern point of view' (Letters, III, pp. 439-40). These matters had become his subject already, however, when he wrote *Nostromo* four years earlier, and they continued to preoccupy him for the rest of his life.

Nostromo is the first to introduce the other, equally 'modern,' topic of 'war and peace,' which for Conrad turns out to mean revolution and its consequences in a post-colonial world.

Eloise Knapp Hay says, "Readers for generations have related Nostromo to Leo Tolstoy's *War and Peace* (1869). The Russian novel may not have been a deliberate model, yet similarities abound: the vast compass of history the two novels re-enact, the celebration of a nation's repulse of an invading army, and the multiple plots and family histories that centre on the making of marriages and the reasons for their success or failure. In *Nostromo,* the families are the Goulds, the Decouds, the Avellanos—all of whom as 'Creoles': that is, South American natives of European descent–and a fourth family, the Italian Violas, who count *Nostromo* as their 'son.' Nostromo is also, again like Tolstoy's novel, a narrative structured by a war of ideas, especially the idea of historical determinism versus individual freedom."

As John Halverson and Ian Watt have shown, following hints in the "Author's Note," Conrad's sense of having a story to tell was sparked by the tale of clever Italian sailor who stole a lighter loaded with silver off the coast of South America ('The Original Nostromo,' pp. 49-52).

With *Nostromo*, Conrad thus turned from his seaman's memories of the Malay Archpelago and Africa to writing about the Western hemisphere, where he had been for many weeks when he was seventeen and eighteen, making three voyages to Caribbean ports and Venezuela in 1875 and 1876. Wars for independence had liberated most of these areas from Spain, and post-independence revolutions were breaking out while Conrad was there.

Conrad begins *Nostromo* with an old folktale, kept alive by the poor in Costaguana, a story of 'two wandering sailors—Americanos, perhaps, but gringos of some sort,' who persuaded 'a gambling, good-for-nothing' Indian to help them find a cursed treasure lying in a desolate ravine (No, p. 4).

A turbulent political history is part of the background of the coastal province of Sulaco, the wealthiest region of the South American republic of Costaguana. Along with the San Tome silver mine, the Englishman Charles Gould has inherited the instability of a civil war between the legal government of Ribiera and the populist party of his military chief Montero. In order to prevent the confiscation of silver by the rebels, Gould is persuaded to entrust it to Martin Decoud, a journalist with ambiguous commitments to the Ribiera government. Decoud is joined by the alien Nostromo ('our man'), the Capataz de Cargadores and a local hero, in smuggling the silver out into the gulf. In the darkness, their loaded lighter is hit and damaged by a rebel troopship; forced to run aground on nearby islands, the Isabels, they conceal the silver and Nostromo returns to Sulaco.

Shocked into awareness by their near-disaster, Nostromo considers how far he has been exploited by his allies, who are aware of his appetite for adventure and glory. Decoud's dilemma is more extreme: his usual skepticism turns to near-madness, and he drowns himself weighted with silver. At this point Nostromo is persuaded to further, desperate heroism by another bearer of disillusionment: Dr Monygham, who was tortured under the previous political regime, and who is in love with Charles Gould's wife, the humane and wise Emilia. Owing to Nostromo's actions in summoning loyal forces, Sulaco and the Goulds are saved from the violence of the rebels.

The ensuing peace proves to be superficial for most characters. Nostromo, who is betrothed to Linda, the daughter of Giorgio Viola, fosters the belief that the silver has been sunk. But he makes clandestine visits to the Isabels, where Giorgio is appointed lighthouse keeper; here, he steals back portions of the silver and finds himself in love with Giselle, the sister of his betrothed. When he is mistaken for an intruder and shot by Giorgio, the secret of the silver is lost for ever.

Many readings of *Nostromo,* and critics like Credic Watts, persuade on of another revolution adumbrated at the end of the novel that has been overlooked. The novel is structured on five ideologies of revolution: Gould's, Giorgio Viola's, the Monterists,' the Marxist's, and a psychological revolution that occurs within Nostromo himself, which calls for more attention than it has received.

Fredric Jameson, going far beyond Irving Howe but in the same direction, finds that in *Nostromo* and all of Conrad's novels, his political vision substitutes romance and drama for the real concerns of life, namely, how we earn our livelihood. Even in Conrad's idealization of shipboard life (which one would think has something to do with earning one's bread), Jameson finds Conrad escaping into a fantasy world, divorced from material reality. Behind his immoderate attacks on Conrad, very similar to Said's, Jameson seems, however, to posit a utopia of his own, a Marxist utopia where physically satisfied lives flourish without illusions concerning non-physical needs. This seems to be as much a fantasy world as any that Conrad constructs, certainly in the very substantial world of *Nostrom.*

The Secret Agent (1907)

In a story called "The Informer" written in January 1906 and published in December of that year, and thus framing the composition of the first draft of *The Secret Agent,* Conrad exposes the political illusions of the *haute bourgeoisie.* The wealthy 'inner' narrator is a connoisseur of Chinese art, of fine cuisine, and of secret political societies; he is also a savagely iconoclastic propagandist of the extreme left, whose support of anarchism is gradually revealed to be yet another form of connoisseurship. His story concerns an upper-society girl who has joined a London anarchist cell in the spirit of a 'high-minded amateur,' and who ends by theatrically rejecting a young comrade whose love for her drives him to confess that he is a police spy.

In the "Author's Note" in 1920 Joseph Conrad writes that he began writing the novel *The Secret Agent* impulsively and continuously. Like some of his other novels the short story "Verloc," gave rise to the novel. *The Secret Agent* was serialized in the American magazine *Ridgway's* in 1907. The novel has 30,000 words length. The revision had coincided with a very difficult, even traumatic, period in Conrad's domestic life: apart from the usual money troubles, he had been racked with anxiety and exhausted with nursing his two sons, who had been seriously ill during a period of residence abroad. As he told Galsworthy, 'It has been altogether a ghastly time.'

The critical reception of the novel was generally favourable, and it was praised in such prestigious weeklies as *The Spectator, The Times Literary Supplement* and *The Nation*. This last review was by Edward Garnett, who delighted Conrad by spotting the significance of Winnie's mother: 'the real heroine of the story is concealed in the trivial figure of Mr Verloc's mother-in-law.' Conrad wrote to him: 'I am no end proud to see you've spotted my poor old woman. You've got a fiendishly penetrating eye for one's most secret intentions. She is the heroine.' However, the novel did not sell. Early in the new year, Conrad told Galsworthy that it 'may be pronounced by now an honourable failure', and confessed that he was cast down.

The Secret Agent shared in the general neglect of Conrad's work during the generation after his death, though Edward Crankshaw suggested in his 1936 book that in it Conrad achieved what may have been the greatest of all his purely technical feats. Its recognition as a masterpiece, and one of the finest of all Conrad's novels, came with the appearance of F. R. Leavis's *The Great Tradition* in 1948, in which Conrad is awarded one of the five places in the pantheon of English fiction and this particular book is declared to be 'one of the two unquestionable classics of the first order that he added to the English novel' (the other is *Nostromo*).

Conrad's manuscript is now in Philadelphia. Towards the end of his life, he made two dramatic versions of *The Secret Agent*: one in four acts was privately printed in 1921, the other in three acts was produced at the Ambassadors' Theatre, London, in 1922. In a letter of 7 November 1906, he stated that the story was based on the inside knowledge of a certain event in the history of active anarchism. In the "Author's Note" of 1920, he offers quite a full account of the origins of the novel. "The subject of *The Secret Agent,* he says there,"... came to me in the shape of a few words uttered by a friend in a casual conversation about anarchists or rather anarchist activities'; the friend was Ford Madox Hueffer, and Conrad adds that, in the course of a discussion on this subject, 'we recalled the already old story of the attempt to blow up the Greenwich Observatory', and that Ford had remarked, 'Oh, that fellow was half an idiot. His sister committed suicide afterwards.' The incident referred to is the so-called 'Greenwich Park Explosion' of 14 February 1894.

The Secret Agent is said to be the history of Winnie Verloc. Although it may have begun as a tale of anarchists with Verloc as a grubby protagonist. (Winnie is less prominent in the serial version than she later became, in its final form). It is arguably a study of relationships in which Winnie is dominant and the anarchist theme sinks into the background. This kind of shift might have seemed to Conrad to justify his repudiation of his earlier debts and would be consistent with Ian Watt's observation that although Joseph Conrad's fiction nearly always started from some germ of reality—an anecdote, an historical event, an incident seen or a conversation overheard—by the time the work was finished it usually disclaimed any relation to actual persons, places or events. While there is in this case a discernible substructure of mysterious and grisly historical events, the most important aspects of the book justify its being regarded as a work of imagination. Norman Page ob erves, "In its evocation of the squalor and brutality of lower-class life in the metropolis, *The Secret Agent* owes something to Dickens, and in its combination of this element with a story of espionage and political intrigue it represents the side of Conrad that was to be an important influence on Graham Greene. The title has a con-sciously lurid quality and seems to offer a different book from the one we are in fact given; the subtitle, 'A Simple Tale,' seems to reinforce, or perhaps to undermine, the title's promise; but we cannot read very far into the book without realizing that both are ironically intended! As a representative of the romantic profession of spy,

Mr Verloc is a joker and, despite its melodramatic surface, the tale turns out to be anything but simple. From the title onwards, indeed, the novel is permeated by a remarkably consistent irony that gives depth and complexity."

As already noted, in some of its aspects—notably its settings—*The Secret Agent* shows the influence of Dickens. In *A Personal Record* Conrad not only refers to a translation of *Nicholas Nickleby* as having been almost his first introduction to English imaginative literature but singles out *Bleak House* for praise as, "a work of the master for which I have such an admiration or rather such an intense and unreasoning affection, dating from the days of my childhood, that its very weaknesses are more precious to me than the strength of other men's works. I have read it innumerable times both in Polish and in English." In his "Author's Note," Conrad describes the way in which the world of *The Secret Agent* imaginatively presented itself to him: "Then the vision of an enormous town presented itself, of a monstrous town more populous than some continents and in its man-made might as if indifferent to heaven's frowns and smiles; a cruel devourer of the world's light. There was room enough there to place any story, depth enough for any passion, variety enough there for any setting, darkness enough to bury five millions of lives."

The novel depicts an urban landscape of dirt and gloom, in which physical objects seem on the point of disintegration and even animate creatures sometimes share this quality. In its opening pages, Mr Verloc's house is grimy, the shop-bell is hopelessly cracked, and his customers' clothes are much worn, and the neighbourhood abounds in narrow alleys and unsavoury courts: we are not far from the foul slum of Tom-All-Alone's in *Bleak House,* though Winnie has been successful in preventing herself and those she loves from being engulfed by the ride of squalor and misery.

Thomas Mann, in his introduction to the German translation of Conrad's works, published in 1926, sees an emphasis in this novel on the contrast between England and Russia and says that the satire against Russian methods comes from a great pride in England's liberty and civilization. It is certainly true that here the English government produces no Mr Vladimirs and that the people of the Embassy deplore the humanitarian bias of the

English authorities and people. But Sir Ethelred, the representative of the British government, and his adoring Toodles are not exempted from a scrutiny of less obvious flaws.

Jacques Berthoud observes, "In this light, Conrad's obsessive defensiveness when writing to his friends about the novel becomes more intelligible, if not more excusable. The main recipients of his letters were variously members of the intellectual left. John Glasworthy, who published the anti-bourgeois *The Man of Property* in 1906, the year during which Conrad was writing *The Secret Agent,* foresaw and welcomed the social revolution which he thought inevitable. In the same year Cunninghame Graham, who had participated in 1889 congress of the Second International and advocated revolution, campaigned as a socialist well to the left of Parliamentary Labour. As for Conrad's literary patron, Edward Garnett, he too was, in Zdzislaw Najder's unsympathetic phrase, a 'leftist liberal' who, with his wife Constance, the greatest English translator of the Russian classics, had long cultivated distinguished anarchist émigrés like Volkhovsky, Kropotkin, and the former assassin Stepniak. There can be no doubt Conrad that held his English friends in the highest regard; but there is also no doubt that he retained his political independence in his relations with them."

Under Western Eyes (1911)

Keith Carabine observes, "Conrad's most succinct and compelling statement about the interdependence of the artist's and of humanity's concerns is contained in a letter to *The New York Times* of 2 August 1901: 'The only legitimate basis of creative work lies in the courageous recognition of all the irreconcilable antagonisms that make our life so enigmatic, so burdensome, so fascinating, so dangerous—so full of hope' (Letters, II pp. 348-9). All his major fictions present, explore, and are constructed out of antagonisms that are never finally resolved."

Two early reviewers of *Under Western Eyes* anticipated the main line of its subsequent critical reception. Conrad's friend Edward Garnett remarked that 'its last page leaves us almost as much in the dark as the first. We can only feel sure that certain actual facts have been presented, and that there is probably an explanation of them if we could only hit upon it.' An anonymous reader observed, 'In more than one way...Mr. Conrad's book belies its title, so deeply tinged is its perceptiveness with Russian habits of thought.'

This familiar Conrdian explanation rest alongside the old teacher's further claim that Russians, anyway, are 'under' his eyes, in that they are 'below' or 'on the inside of' and are therefore incomprehensible to him because of their remote racial and historical traditions and 'the different conditions of Western thought' (p. 25).

The narrator, an elderly English teacher of languages in Geneva, tells the story of the Russian student Razumov, using Razumov's diary as well as his own observation.

Razumov's quiet life in St Petersburg is disrupted when Victor Haldin, a revolutionary idealist who has just assassinated a minister of state, seeks shelter with him. He betrays Haldin to the police, only to find that the autocracy now regards him as a suspect. His isolation intensifies when he is dispatched to Geneva as a secret agent. He arrives with the reputation of a hero among his fellow Russian exiles, since Haldin had written admiringly about him to his mother and young sister, Natalia. Natalia's innocent devotion to the man she thinks tried to help her brother makes Razumov's guilt the harder to bear. He is repelled, further, by the cynical idealism of the revolutionaries, epitomized in the grotesque figure of Peter Ivanovitch. When he attempts to break free from his life of deceit, confessing both to Natalia and to the revolutionaries, he brings ghastly retribution on himself. They burst his eardrums, and he is struck down and crippled by a tram he cannot hear.

In *Under Western Eyes* the shadow of autocracy lies on the Russians and on Razumove, darkening his figure to the narrator's understanding (p. 184). Its 'destructive reach is inescapable, 'tingeing' Russian thoughts, views, and feelings, and terribly, 'haunting the secret of her silences' (p. 107). Razumov, especially, is tinged. After Haldin's disruption, hi case is tragic because he has to identify himself as a Russian because otherwise, as a friendless orphan, he had nothing. With nowhere to go to he is obliged to make a choice between the warring forces of autocracy and revolution. He chooses the former because as he angrily tells Mikulin, punning on his name (*razum* is the Russian root for reason), 'I am reasonable' (p. 89). He therefore prizes 'the secular logic of human development' that Haldin, like all 'Visionaries,' holds in contempt (p. 95). Razumov's liberating providential plot manifests his desire to escape 'the comedy of errors' that he feels is orchestrated by the devil.

Freya of the Seven Isles (1902)

This appeared in the *Metropolitan Magazine* and in *the London Magazine* in 1912. It had been completed in 1911, and on the fifteenth of that month Conrad had described it in a letter to Warrington Dawson as 'quite good magazine stuff, quite Conradesque.'

Freya is a beautiful motherless girl who, like Alice in "A Smile of Fortune," has very long hair; she lives on an island with her weak and unworldly father, a Dane called Nielsen. Jasper Alien, the owner of a trading brig, the *Bonito,* falls in love with her, and they plan to elope as soon as she reaches the age of twenty-one and to live happily ever after on the gleaming white boat that is 'fitted-up-like-a-gentleman' and yacht and is Jasper's pride and joy. But a brutal Dutch naval lieutenant, Heemskirk, who commands a gunboat, becomes attracted to Freya and, possessed by jealousy of Jasper, contrives that the yacht is seized and run aground on a reef and the young man charged wrongfully with gun-running. Grieved by the loss of his boat, Jasper sinks into a kind of lethargy; and the girl falls ill and dies of pneumonia. Freya is a kind of Eve-figure or mythological being (at one point she is addressed as ' "You Scandinavian Goddess of Love"); and the life she hopes to live with Jasper has an idealized, otherworldly quality.

S. K. Land thinks "Freya of the Seven Isles" presents a heroine victimized by a father and a lover.

Chance (1913)

S. K. Land observes, "Conrad's third phase comprises *Chance,* Victory, *The Shadow Line* and number of contemporary short stories. In this phase, Conrad seeks non-involvement in the conflicts of life, but one who does so selflessly and harmlessly by simply withdrawing into isolation. There are no victims to this neutrality, no Decouds, Haldins, Teresas, or elderly widows. On the contrary, the new heroes, far from sacrificing others to their need for security, compromise themselves from motives of humanity in order to alleviate sufferings which they might, without risk to themselves, have left behind them. The heroes of the second phase compromised their neutrality against their will under pressure of circumstances, but the new heroes, Anthony, Heyst and Renouard, deviate from their policy of isolation in order to effect the rescue of a fellow creature, who is usually the heroine."

The essential feature of the third phase is the hero's tendency to retreat into isolation or inactivity and his compromise of this withdrawal in undertaking a purposive course of action, consisting usually in the actual or attempted rescue of the heroine. The rescue motif is not essential to these stories, for the hero's compromising undertaking may, as in *The Shadow-Line*, be altogether of another kind. It does not occur in most of them, however, and is no less prominent in the novels of the fourth and final phase.

The development of the rescue motif in Conrad's fiction has its roots in the heroines of political stories. Conrad's interest in his heroines grew steadily from his first attempt at a plausible and morally significant female character of Emilia Gould. Winnie Verloc and Natalia Haldin continue a rising theme, that of the innocent and generally well-intentioned woman entrapped. Between the completion of *Under Western Eyes* and *The Secret Sharer* at the end of 1999, and that of *Chance* in 1912. Conrad wrote four shorter pieces. Two of these, *Prince Roman* and *The Partner* are brief and casual tales with no bearing on the major works, but the others, A *Smile of Fortune* and *Freya of the Seven Isles*, longer and more careful stories, both take up the theme of the beleaguered female, which was to dominate *Chance* and *Victory*.

Both are concerned with marriageable daughters who are in the care of morally weak and socially isolated fathers and are sought after by passing sea-captains, who in the end fail them, an outline which, apart from the final failure, might also be abstracted from *Chance*.

Common to both these stories and to *Chance* is the pivotal triangle of heroine, lover and father, with the father as a dangerously selfish figure largely responsible for the heroine's difficulties. The theme of *Chance* however, is a new departure for Conrad, arising from the increasing importance of his heroines since Emilia. Here he turns for his conceptual framework from politics to sexuality. The dualistic conflict in *Chance* arises not from the struggle of conservative and radical ideologies but from the encounter of masculine and feminine principles.

The hero and heroine of *Chance* are Captain Roderick Anthony and Flora de Barral, but a logical account of the structure of its plot begins not with them but with their respective fathers, Carleon Anthony and De Barral the financier, for it is these two men who establish the conceptual polarity in terms of which the story is conducted. Carleon Anthony, dead before the tale begins, had two children, both of whom ran away and deserted him as soon as they were old enough to do so, namely, Roderick, the hero, and Zoe, known in the story as the feminist, Mrs. Fyne. Conrad writes, "The late Carleon Anthony, the poet, sang in his time, of the domestic and social amenities of our age with a most felicitous versification, his object being, in his own words 'to glorify the result of six hundred years.' I don't know. His poems read like sentimental novels told in verse of a really superior quality" (p.38).

De Barral, the heroine's father does much business and attracts much investment. If Carleon Anthony is known for his poetry, De Baral is known for his advertisement. Conrad writes of De Barral's advertisement thus: "One remembers his first modest advertisements headed with the magic word Thrift, Thrift, Thrift, thrice repeated: promising ten percent on all deposits and giving the address of the Thrift and Independence And Association in Vauxhall Bridge Road. Apparently nothing more was necessary" (p. 79).

Conrad depicts both figures Carleon Anthony and De Barral as insincere people. Carleon's poetry is a kind of nonsense verse. Carleon's son, the hero, runs away to sea in reaction against his father, and the daughter becomes a feminist and marries mild and unpoetic man, the "pedestrian" John Fyne, of whom her father disapproves. De Barral is similarly expose as fraud, in a more technically legal sense of the term, when his financial empire collapses, involving many people in extensive losses. De Barral himself is prosecuted, convicted and sentenced to imprisonment for his conduct, a process which draws his daughter, Flora, through a sequence of traumatic experience.

S. K. Land observes, "The opposition between idealism and material acquisition displayed in a somewhat caricature fashion in the persons of Carleon Anthony and De Barral, is prominent in much of Conrad's earlier work. The contradictory heroes of the first mature phase frequently exhibit both idealistic and materialistic impulses."

In such a background, the two great men's children inherit much dualistic materialism. So Roderick Anthony and Flora de Barral come together. Captain Anthony "was the son of a poet with a considerable gift of individualizing of etherealizing the common place; of making touching, delicate, fascinating the most hopeless conventions of the so-called, refined existence" (p. 193). The inheritance manifests itself in a deliberate cultivation of high minded rectitude in Anthony's relations with Flora, an unworldly attitude which in him, as in his father, is an outgrowth of eccentricity.

The outcome is that, when Anthony takes action in pursuit of his heroine, his inherited idealism drives him into a stand of artificial and strained magnanimity, the arrangement whereby Flora is to be his wife in name only. In a very similar way Flora, who believes that De Barral is "the only human being that really cared for her" (p. 380) enters into this arrangement for her father's sake and marries Anthony initially in order to secure shelter and protection for De Barral on his release from prison.

This marriage is a marriage of compromise. Flora's marriage is like Winnie's marriage to Verloc for the sake of Stevie. The hero and heroine are the central pair of counterbalanced characters in the story. There are a number of parallels between their situations; both lost their family life in early youth and were brought up by distant relations; both are friendless persons.

However, AnthonyFlora's marriage is further complicated by other events and characters. Characters like Flora's Governess, Mrs. Fyne, Captain Anthony's sister, each of them interfere with Anthony-Flora relationship. The Governess calls Flora unloveable; Mrs. Fyne observes that Flora does not love Anthony; and similar situations complicate the hero-heroine's relations. Anthony's "vanity" is his inheritance from the "aristocrat" (p. 72) father, an exaggerated sense of chivalric dignity which drives him to make his magnanimous offer to Flora.

The reaction of Flora, who has up to this time believed in and enjoyed Anthony's love, is one of bitter chill. Anthony's offer appears to her as coldness, as a rejection of her person confirming the words of the Governess which she had never been able to forget. The reciprocal compromises of Anthony and Flora are thus the products of influences exerted by two pairs of secondary characters.

So the couple become each other's nemesis. If the husband thinks his wife, a woman is a weak character, she just wants his money not his love. They stand on equal footing. Critic Land observes, "The structural symmetry of *Chance* does not stop with the three pairs of counterbalanced characters we have so far observed. Each of the third pair (both women) is connected to a male, who exercises a faintly ameliorating influence upon his partner's actions. The Governess is associated with the young man Charley, whom she hoped to marry, for mercenary reasons, to Flora, and who shows some sympathy for the girl by cutting short the Governess' parting verbal attack. Very similarly, Mrs. Fyne's husband, John, is only reluctantly his wife."

A final pair of characters emerges in the last phase of the story aboard the *Ferndale*. An alignment is established here in which the first mate, Franklin, takes the Captain's side against Flora and her father, while Powell, the second mate, befriends the newcomers and finds himself out of sympathy with Franklin's attitude. The remainder of the crew share Franklin's view; he is their spokesman and the only one of them to appear as a named character. Franklin idolizes Anthony and jealously resents the unhappiness which, not knowing the full story, he believes that Flora has brought upon the Captain. Powell takes Flora's part. This does not involve him in opposition to Anthony, to whom he is completely loyal, but it is none the less true that Powell later replaces, first, Franklin as chief mate and, later, Anthony himself, as Flora's husband.

But the character Marlow remains neutral to the whole story. The dynamite cargo of the *Ferndale* is emblematic of the potentially explosive state of tension created by the joint compromise of Anthony and Flora. The ship is the world to which they have withdrawn in pursuit of their ideal, a normal marital relationship, much as Jim withdraws to Patusan, Whaley to the *Sofala,* and Razumov to Geneva.

The situation aboard the *Ferndale* seems all set to conclude with a bang, as do the comparable situations in most of Conrad's other works-*An Outcast of the Islands, Lord Jim, The End of the Tether, Under Western Eyes,* and *Victory* for instance in all of which the hero perishes in some kind of detonation, collision, or combustion. Yet in *Chance* the apocalypse is largely averted.

Chance in fact, presents a less gloomy view of life. Conrad here became an optimist, thereby winning a popular success for the novel. So the story ends in a happy note.

We notice that De Barrals's role is reduced in the end, felicitating Anthony-Flora's happy life. But in the second round of voyage on *Westland,* Anthony is shipwrecked. Anthony is the hero of Chance and is a typical hero of the third phase. He is initially, like Heyst and Renouard, a recluse who has withdrawn from a troubled world, in this case to a placid but successful life at sea. He compromises this retreat, very much as does Heyst, in order to effect the rescue of the heroine, who like Lena, is being victimized by the world.

Chance has multiple narrations. Both Marlow and Powell also act as narrators making the narrative complex. A second, but closely related reason for the technical complexity of *Chance* is the need to unify what would otherwise be a broad and far-ranging story. The inclusion of Marlow as collector and narrator of most of this information within the frame of Powell's two part story of his own association with Anthony's ship results in all well polished formal unity. Marlow is allowed to play an integral part in Flora's life within the story as, first, her savior from attempted suicide and, later, the agent who negotiates her marriage to Powell.

Victory (1915)

Robert Hampson observes, "The novel begins with an unnamed narrator who is identified only as one of us 'out there' (p. 3). He claims no direct knowledge of Heyst, but pieces together his narrative about him from the gossip of Europeans in the Malay Archipelago and, in particular, by following Davidson's investigations into Heyst's disappearance. Only in Part II is there a shift to Heyst's perspective and a revelation of his inner world. The unnamed narrator had drawn attention to Heyst's reserve, courtesy, and gentlemanliness, but Part II reveals the programme of drift, the 'system of restless wandering' that Heyst has adopted as a way of 'passing through life without suffering' (p. 90)."

The story is set in Indonesia. On a rare impulse the solitary and cynical Axel Heyst helps Morrison, the captain of a trading brig, by paying his fines. He is offered a share in the Tropical Belt Coal Company and becomes its owner when Morrison dies. The Company fails but Heyst remains on the island of Samburan, alone except for his servant Wang. Schomberg, the hotel keeper in Sourabaya, circulates rumours that Heyst murdered Morrison and has secreted a fortune on the island. His malignancy increases when Heyst, on a rare visit, rescues an English girl, Lena, from his unwanted attentions and takes her home with him. Schomberg invites a trio of desperadoes to raid Heyst's island: the woman-hating 'plain Mr Jones', his 'secretary' Ricardo, and the Caliban-like Pedro. Found by Ricardo, Lena feigns sympathy for his plan to steal the illusory fortune. Jones finds her with Ricardo and fires at him; he dies and Lena is mortally wounded. Jones drowns while trying to escape from the island. Lena dies in Heyst's arms with the smile of private 'victory' on her lips. Heyst commits suicide in despair; the bungalow in which Lena dies becomes their joint pyre.

Joseph Conrad's brilliance stems from his experience and insights into man's life. His use of English is wonderful. "His genius lies partly in his penetrating sense of the human ordeal and in his infusion of psychological insight. He rigorously disciplined his admittedly romantic temperament with an unsparing moral judgment." Conrad's artistry lies in his exceptional style and craftsmanship. His style is a creation of both psychological and poetic strength.

The Shadow-Line (1917)

Schwarz in his *Conrad: The Later Fiction* thinks that One of the late works that has not followed the pattern of neglect and undervaluation is *The Shadow-Line*. F.R. Leavis, in 1958, for example, described it as 'central to Conrad's genius.' This is perhaps the same as saying that, although it was written in 1915, it is, in many ways, a return to 'old subjects' and old methods. Conrad described it to his agent, J.B. Pinker, as old subject something in the style of Youth.' As in 'Youth,' the story is based directly on Conrad's own experience: in this case, his command of the Otago in 1888. But, unlike, 'Youth,' its narration is not staged as a tale-within-a-tale; instead, like 'The Secret Sharer,' it presents a narrator's first-person reminiscence. Like that story, too, it is concerned with the loneliness of first command, and the account of a journey is used to describe an earlier self's progress 'from innocence to experience and from youth to maturity."

As Frederick Karl has pointed out in his biography of Conrad, after *Victory*, completed in 1914 and published in the following year, 'all of Conrad's work was an extension of *A Personal Record*—that is to say, it was either explicitly offered as reminiscences or, in the case of the novels and short stories, was fictionalized autobiography, a reliving and reshaping of his own earlier experience." Karl adds that the unevenness of this work resulted chiefly from Conrad's inability to turn personal experience into creative materials. Still Conrad's *Shadow Line* is a masterly work, demanding enough critical appreciation. He himself made no secret of its origins: a letter to John Quinn ascribes it as a sort of autobiography. Its origins go back a full generation to 1888, when Conrad quit the *Vidar* and, at a loose end in Singapore, was unexpec-tedly given the command of the *Otago* and went forthwith to Bangkok to take up his first command. He retained the Gulf of Siam as his setting in the story and stayed close to the events and even the names of those involved in his experience. There are strong resemblances between *The Shadow-Line* and Conrad's slightly earlier story "The Secret Sharer."

Conrad began work on *The Shadow-Line* in 1915. It is thus a wartime story, and its dedication to Borys Conrad, his son, who was serving in the armed forces, as well as to the other young men of his generation, brings together the experience of the two generations of father and son. It was serialized in the *English Review* and in the *Metropolitan* (New York) in 1916, and appeared in volume form in 1917. Writing in the *Sphere* the well-known critic Clement Shorter took the opportunity to note that Conrad had now arrived as a popular as well as a critically esteemed writer. An anonymous reviewer in the *Nation* described the book as 'written at Mr Conrad's fullest imaginative stretch.'

The title is explicated both in the dedication and in the story itself: ". . . the time, too, goes on till one perceives ahead a shadow-line warning one that the region of early youth, too, must be left behind." F. R. Leavis says in his fine essay on *The Shadow-Line* in Anna Karenina and Other Essays (1967), 'The ship and the command are, for the young Captain, a symbol and a test: the experience in the Gulf of Siam is an ordeal. When the new captain sees his ship for the first time, his 'feeling of emptiness' is suddenly replaced by 'a flow of joyous emotion,' and that joy is not destroyed by the bitter difficulties with which he is soon confronted.

The hero felt at that time that "There was nothing original, new, startling, informing to expect from the world: no opportunities to find out something about oneself, no wisdom to acquire, no fun to enjoy" (p.23). He talks of his "deep attachment from the forms and colours of this world" (p. 35), a feeling of withdrawal which persists well after he has put to sea and which is vanquished only at the successful conclusion of the first voyage. Like Anthony, Heyst and Renouard, the Captain is unable to maintain his chosen course of isolation. Yet he is in the end persuaded to take the offered command.

This is his compromise, corresponding to Heyst's rescues of Morrison and Lena, to Renouard's engagement of Arthur, and to Anthony's involvement with Flora. The compromise does not, in this case, include a rescue, except in the rather tenuous sense that the hero's acceptance of the command rescues the stranded ship after its previous master's demise.

The Captain, persuaded back into participation in life, follows a course generally similar to that of Heyst. He first provokes a rival, in this case the supercilious Hamilton, who attempts to snatch the command from under his nose. Hamilton, however, is easily defeated and plays only a small part in the story.

The Captain confronts his destiny on a ship at sea with a particular assistance of two of his officers. The Captain's reluctant parting with Ransome is significant of his own conquest of the impulse to withdraw fearfully from life.

The Shadow Line exhibits the fundamentals of the Conradian fictional pattern. The hero, the Captain, adopts an ideal, in this case the pursuit of indolent detachment, but compromises by accepting a command and thereafter oscillates between the poles of the novel's dualistic conceptual framework.

The Shadow-Line begins with the narrator's younger self going through a period of crisis, which is presented as characteristic of 'that twilight region between youth and maturity' (SL, p. 26).

The Shadow-Line recounts a rite of passage into mature identity within the male world of Merchant Navy. This, however, is not the only border with which the story is concerned. There are also the 'Shadow-lines' between sanity and madness, the natural and the supernatural, and life and death.

The Shadow Line belongs to Conrad's third phase because the hero who attempts to retreat from involvement and responsibility.

Two critics, Cox and Leavis show another significant difference of interpretation. For Cox, although this is Conrad's last masterpiece, it is a simpler, less resonant work than "The Secret Sharer": whereas that is typical of Conrad's modernism and a story of questioning and uncertainty about the grounds of being and action, *The Shadow-Line* is comparatively straightforward and ends with the test satisfactorily completed. For Leavis, on the other hand, "The Secret Sharer"undertakes much less than *The Shadow-Line* does, and the latter is a profound work, and complex in its profundity.

The Arrow of Gold (1919)

Conrad wrote this novel quite rapidly. The dedication is to Richard Curie. To some extent *The Arrow of Gold* is a reworking of Conrad's unfinished novel *The Sisters* (published posthumously), the heroine of which shares a name and much else with the heroine of the later book. Conrad also reworked material that had appeared in the penulti-mate chapter ('The Tremolino") of *The Mirror of the Sea*, though a significant difference between the two versions is aptly noted by Frederick Karl: The novel is the obverse of the "Tremolino" in *The Mirror of the Sea*, as if additional retrospect had bleached out the adventure and brought into relief the romance.

The action of the novel is set in the 1870s, some forty years earlier than the date of composition in the period of Conrad's own youth. He had been in Marseilles, where the action takes place, in 1877-8, but the novel is set in 1875—a more exciting moment in history, since at that time the Carlist war was still in progress and there was still some possibility that the Pretender would obtain the throne. Civil war over the Carlist question in Spain had been recommenced in 1870 by Don Carlos, grandson of the original claimant to the throne; he suffered military defeats in 1872 and 1874, and in 1876 and was forced to seek exile in France.

The Arrow of Gold begins with the hero, George, in a situation typical of the Conradian protagonist at the outset of his adventures. He is a wanderer at a loose end, a seaman ashore after a long voyage with no clear plans for the future. The disengaged hero is known as "Young Ulysses." Conrad connects this story with *The Shadow Line* by calling it a tale of initiation. George is fascinated by an Englishman called Mills, whose role corresponds closely to that of Captain Giles in *The Shadow Line*. Mills is a somewhat older man, worldly and well-connected, whom the hero respects and admires.

So Mills in *The Arrow of Gold* is the deliberate means of George's association with the dangerous Carlist cause.

It is Mills who introduces George to Blunt, together with whom he has decided that George "should be drawn into the affair if it could be done" (p.5); Blunt and Mills together then take George to meet Rita. The cause of which George commits himself, in a context which looks back to the political novels of Conrad's middle period, is Carlism, the movement to restore the Bourbon Don Carlos to the throne of Spain.

Against George, who represents to Rita honesty, simplicity and ease, stands Ortega, to whom she is bound by ties of background, family and religion. Her pious sister, Ortega's advocate, constantly reinforces the bond. Ortega is in many ways George's opposite. The dilemma Rita faces, caught between George and Ortega, is broadly similar to that which George himself experiences between the ways represented by Dominic and Blunt.

Both George and Rita therefore stand as protagonists in the story, each flanked by one or more pairs of opposing characters whose contrary tendencies indicate conflicts of choice and moral dilemmas. Another established role, that of the anti-heroine also reappears in *The Arrow of Gold,* although the character, Therese is not paired in any obvious way with an opposite figure. Therese occupies a position in *The Arrow of Gold* close to that of the anti-heroine of the early stories.

The novel has an important autobiographical basis, and its protagonist, Monsieur George, has much in common with the young Conrad, who was known in Marseilles as 'Monsieur Georges.' Conrad wrote in a letter (16 January 1921) that his correspondent's surmise that Mr George of *The Arrow of Gold* is in a sense myself is just', but due weight needs to be given to that saving phrase 'in a sense.' The serious weaknesses of the novel have been generally recognized: it is slow-moving and portentous, and the principal characters never really come to life. Some have taken the view that the weakness of the novel is a symptom of the general decline of Conrad's powers in his later year. His original plan involved narrating the story, wholly or in part, through a series of letters written by the protagonist to a woman he had known in his youth, the protagonist being a man of about Conrad's own age. This structure gives the novel its subtitle, 'A Story between Two Notes.'

Most of Part I is taken up with a discussion between Mills and Blunt, to which M. George listens, which presents a series of images and impressions of Rita. Rita's reification is signaled by the role of the painter and collector Allegre in her life. Through his patronage and through the dialogue betweens Mills and Blunt about its consequences Rita is presented as an object for consumption and/or exchange—as the aesthetic object of the male gaze, as the sexual object of male desire, and as an image in a discourse between males. Her objectification is confirmed by her 'double,' the dummy that stood in for her during Allegre's painting sessions, which continues to act as a surrogate for her for both M. Geogre and the reader. In addition, this 'mutilated dummy' (p. 122) suggests both the implicit sadism of the male gaze and Rita's role as the body upon which male spectators project various roles and identities.

The Second Note similarly opens the end of the novel into a range of questions. While it presents a picture of idyllic 'precarious bliss,' it leaves open the possibility that this 'bliss' is merely a projection of M. George's, and that he is, unknown to himself, merely another appropriating male rather than the ideal lover that he sees himself as in his narrative. Whatever the answer, in this Second Note, the figure of Rita disappears behind successive veils until we are left with a final exchange between M. George and Mills. According to Mills, Rita has 'sacrificed' her chance love to the 'integrity' of M. George's life. There is, however, always the possibility, as Roberts has argued, that Mills is telling M. George what he feels M. George needs to hear or, even, that Mills has failed to understand that Rita has acted to protect her own integrity.

Contemporary reception of the novel was mixed. Apparently hypnotised by Conrad's successes earlier in the decade and his new-found fame, a few reviewers bestowed praise on it that makes one gasp: Sir Sidney Colvin described it as 'a study of a woman's heart and mystery scarcely to be surpassed in literature' and an anonymous reviewer in the *Morning Post* found it 'an extraordinarily fascinating work'. Others were less enthusiastic, but it was generally treated with respect, and Sherry notes that 'With the publication of *The Arrow of Gold,* Conrad became the grand old man of letters, taking over the mantle of Thomas Hardy' - an accolade explicitly bestowed by the *New Statesman.*

The Rescue (1920)

Originally titled *The Rescuer: a Tale of Narrow Waters,* it was serialized in *Land and Water* and in the New York magazine *Romance* in 1919 and 1920. As the dates of English serialization indicate, it was not completed until a fairly late stage of the serial run. Volume publication, with the subtitle "A Romance of the Shallows," followed in 1920. The dedication is to Frederic Coutland Penfield, the United States Ambassador to Vienna who had helped the Conrads to escape from Austria after they had been trapped on the Continent by the outbreak of war in 1914. The text was extensively revised between serialization and volume publi-cation, and incorporates suggestions made by Garnett.

In fact the outline of *The Rescue* was clear in his mind from the beginning, as shown by the sketch he gave of it in a letter to William Blackwood in 1897.

The human interest of the tale is in the contact of Lingard, the simple, masterful, imaginative adventurer with a type of civilized woman—a complex type. He is a man tenacious of purpose, enthusiastic in undertaking, faithful in friendship. He jeopardizes the success of his plans first to assure her safety and then absolutely sacrifices them to what he believes the necessary condition of her happiness. He is throughout mistrusted by the whites whom he wishes to save; he is unwittingly forced into a context with his Malay friends. Then when the rescue, for which he had sacrificed all the interests of his life, is accomplished he has to face his reward an inevitable separation. This episode of his lift lifts him out of himself.

Lingard's initial compromise, sketched lightly and retrospectively in *The Rescue,* is closely akin to those of the early heroes. It seems that he, like Willems, tired of lowly status and drudgery among his own people, took to slightly dishonest means (in his case some form of smuggling or piracy) as an easy way to independence and found himself, as a result cast out from the white world and obliged to find a new arena for his activities among blacks.

The result of Lingard's life as an adventurer is his involvement with Malay natives, both because he is no longer acceptable among whites and because, in a moment of danger on strange shore, he falls under obligation to the Rajah Hassim, who saves his life. His debt to Hassim in turn embroils Lingard in native politics, for when the Rajah is deposed and exiled the hero undertakes to organize a military alliance for the accomplishment of his restoration.

The Rescue returns to the world of Conrad's earliest novels, *Almayer's Folly* and *An Outcast of the Islands;* and its protagonist had already appeared in the latter novel. The Lingard of *The Rescue* is younger than the Lingard of *An Outcast,* just as *An Outcast* had depicted an earlier phase of his life than appears in *Almayer's Folly;* thus the three novels form, in Frederick R. Karl's apt phrase, 'a special kind of trilogy in reverse chronological order.' In a letter of 1919, Conrad wrote: 'It may well be that [*The Rescue*] . .. will remain the swansong of *Romance* as a literary art.' Certainly its themes and techniques are those to which he had been favourably disposed throughout his career. About its success there have been wide difference of opinion. Baines finds it, though 'unashamedly romantic', 'a work of considerable merit'; he praises the depiction of Lingard as hero and the 'firm moral pivot' of the story. The interest of the action hinges on the conflict in Lingard's mind between his pledge to Hassim and his obligation to save the lives of the people from the stranded yacht. Baines finds Mrs Travers, with whom Lingard falls in love, 'one of Conrad's few convincing female portraits.'

Conrad's reputation by this time can be estimated from the fact that 20, 000 copies of the first edition were printed. Contemporary reviewers were enthusiastic and even fulsome: one found the novel 'so massive, so profound, so beautiful,' while another judged it Conrad's masterpiece. An interesting review in the *Times Literary Supplement,* which seems to be by Virginia Woolf, discusses Conrad as a romantic writer and reaches the conclusion that in this novel he has attempted a romantic theme and in the middle his belief in romance has failed him.

The Rover (1923)

Robert Hampson observes, "Where *The Arrow of Gold* features 'young Ulysses,' *The Rover,* begun in October 1921 and finished in July 1922, represents a sailor's homecoming. The narrative begins with the return to France of Jean Peyrol after a lifetime spent at sea. Like Rita de Lastola and Flora de Barral, he has passed through an experience in childhood that has decisively shaped his character. In his case, the early traumatic experience, the death of his mother, has led to emotional self-concealment as a way of accepting 'the new and inexplicable conditions of life' (p. 25)."

Conrad's last completed novel, is, like *Suspense,* a historical novel set in the Napoleonic period. A date on the manuscript indicates that work on *The Rover* began early in 1921. As so often with Conrad, the scale of the original conception was considerably more modest than the eventual outcome. In the early months of 1922 Conrad suffered periods of illness, but work on *The Rover* continued, portions of it being dictated. Progress was still slow, and by late April only the first six chapters had been dispatched to Pinker. Then things improved, and Conrad finished the novel in the same year. Composition was still a painful business for Conrad.

Peyrol, the hero, like George and Lingard before him, is a sympathetic pirate, a sea adventurer. His character was formed under the sun of the Indian Seas in lawless contests in his kind for little loot that vanished as soon as grasped, but mainly for bare life almost as precarious to hold through its ups and downs (p.1). His real life, as a member of the notorious Brotherhood of the Coast establishes one pole of his existence, his freedom and his association with the sea. The other pole, which becomes prominent as the story develops, is his patriotism, his commitment to the land, in his case to France, the country of his birth.

The story opens with Peyrol's compromise, his attempt to balance together these two conflicting impulses by retiring to the place of his origin to live quietly on the proceeds of his piracy. "Loot big or little was a natural fact of his freebooter's life" (p.13), and Peyrol had suddenly and unexpectedly found himself in possession of a considerable treasure in gold. To enjoy this in peace he decides to live ashore and, at the same time, to satisfy his "instinct of rest" by settling in the place where he had been born. The indecisive ambivalent nature of his retreat is imaged in the place he chooses, for although it is a farmhouse on land it is also situated on a peninsula and is therefore surrounded on three sides by the sea. His room gives him the sense of "being in a lighthouse.... Not a bad place for a seaman to live in" (p.30). The compromise is further represented in Peyrol's purchase of a boat, a tartane, which he keeps in a nearby cove ready for sea, although he never takes it any distance.

Peyrol's tartan reflects the old man's hovering between two lives yet committed to neither. He has left the sea, but has not yet fully surrendered to the claims of the land.

The dramatic structure of this tale despite its differences from the other two, is broadly the same three part arrangement that is to be seen in *The Arrow of Gold* and *The Rescue.*

In the shorter second movement the hero confronts his rival and wins his heroine. The final movement features the action of the memesis, represented in *The Rover* by Real, the French officer whose place Peyrol takes on the fatal mission.

It is perhaps no more than coincidental that Conrad's career as a novelist closes in a major key with the ending of *The Rover,* one of his few stories and his only full length novel apart from *The Shadow Line* in which the hero succeeds in his object and balances satisfactorily his own account with fate. Peyrol dies in the process, but he does so willingly, under no compulsion beyond his feeling for Arlette and his patriotism and he is, besides, an old man whose natural course has been run. Peyrol's age is crucial to the tone of the novel.

The novel was published in 1922, with a dedication to G. Jean-Aubry. Conrad's status as a best-seller by this stage in his career may be measured by the size of the British edition, which was 40 000 copies. Sales were very good, its American success no doubt being helped (as Najder points out) by the recent sale in New York of Quinn's collection of Conrad's manuscripts, which had attracted widespread publicity. Najder writes: "The reception given *The Rover* was, all in all, the reverse of how Conrad's books had been received twenty-five or fifteen years earlier: now popular acclaim and sales were high, while the voices of the reviewers were cool and censorious." It is true that Raymond Mortimer in the *New Statesman* judged it 'downright bad' and remarked acidly that 'contact with [Conrad's] mind does not seem to me a delight in itself; that Leonard Woolf described it as 'melodramatic'; that the *Glasgow Evening News* found it 'a disappointment.'

Peyrol, the protagonist is an old man who has been a master gunner in the French Navy. Following an instinct of rest, he has settled in a lonely inn near Toulon. Jean-Aubry aptly draws attention to the significance of Conrad's portrayal, near the end of his life, of an elderly sailor whose only desire is for rest; and it is touching to reflect that the epigraph of the novel, two lines from Spenser, were soon to be used again on Conrad's tombstone. Najder notes that, "this was the only book written in the closing years of his life which engaged many of the author's deepest sentiments: his nostalgia for the Mediterranean, his dislike of revolution, and his acquired English patriotism which is in constant contrast to the austere and yet spontaneous attachment to man's native soil shown by the novel's French hero." Conrad himself described the book to Garnett as 'a thing of sentiment.'

While assuredly a minor novel, it has not been unadmired, Baines for instance regarding it as 'a worthy swansong' and suggesting that 'the writing shows no decline in power.'

Geddes in his work *Conrad's Late Novels* thinks that Conrad's description of *The Rover* as 'a feat of artistic brevity' is most obviously witnessed in the economic handling of narrative. The 'intensity and concreteness' of the images, the narrative 'tautness,' and the way in which the novel's final pages are 'the culmination of a movement that builds from the earliest descriptions of character and place in the novel' have been rightly praised.

***Suspense* (1925)**

It remained unfinished at Conrad's death, some 80, 000 words existing of what was evidently to have been a long novel. It was serialized in the *Saturday Review of Literature* in 1925, and published in volume form in the same year.

Subtitled "A Napoleonic Novel," *Suspense* occupied Conrad on and off for about twenty years. In *Joseph Conrad: The Making of a Novelist* (1940), John D. Gordan reminds us that, even though Conrad based so much of his fiction on first-hand experience, he also drew heavily on printed sources, and many episodes in his novels are based on his reading. For *Suspense* he pursued his researches into the Napoleonic period, and during some of the rather rare holidays he took from writing for instance, in Capri in 1905, in Montpellier in 1907, and in Corsica in 1921—he read histories and memoirs, as well as seeking out material in the British Museum. The short story "The Warrior's Soul" was a minor offshoot of these researches, and the novel *The Rover* a more substantial byproduct. An important source, from which Conrad seems to have derived his plot, was the *Memoirs of the Comtesse de Boigne.*

Conrad told Hueffer that the story was to end with Napoleon's departure from Elba; apart from this, his intentions for the unwritten portion are unknown. In a letter to his agent Pinker in 1924, a few months before his death, he described it as 'a biggish thing' and predicted that those who had found *The Rover* rather slight would find weight and body enough in what's coming. When the book appeared, Garnett responded to an adverse review in the *New Statesman,* in which the reviewer had declared that it 'does not come to life at all,' by declaring that it was 'a pure work of art' and 'the most mature of all Conrad's works.' An interesting review that maintains a careful balancing act between praise and blame is that by Leonard Woolf, reprinted in *Critical Heritage.* Woolf found in it 'many of Conrad's great merits' and judged the characters typically Conradian, but was left, despite its solidity and seriousness, with a strong feeling of emptiness and hollowness.

The Sisters (1928)

Conrad began *The Sisters* in the autumn of 1895, shortly after completing his second novel, *An Outcast of the Islands.* He worked on it for several months and by March 1896 had written about 10,000 words; then he abandoned it, apparendy on the advice of Edward Garnett, and turned to the novel that later became *The Rescue.* Garnett felt that Conrad was not getting to grips with the story and was anxious to guide him back to a sphere which he really knew so that he could both develop his talent and at the same time have some likelihood of a popular success. The action of the novel was to have been set in Passy, the district of Paris in which Marguerite Poradowska lived. The novel in seven chapters is an essay on Byronism. The hero is a young painter named Stephen who has come from the Ukraine and settled in Paris. A second line of action concerns a young girl Rita, who has left her Basque village to come to Paris. The name Rita was later to be used in *The Arrow of Gold.* Evidently the two were to meet; presumably they were to fall in love; and apparently the story was to end tragically. The rest, as Baines says, must be guess work. Baines also notes that the style of the fragment is in places 'bizarrely stilted and lifeless,' and its abandonment is probably no great loss. *The Sisters* was published in 1928, four years after Conrad's death, with an introduction by Ford Madox Ford.

If then, Conrad's last novels return to old subjects, it is to the concern with women and sexuality that featured in his earliest works, *Almayer's Folly* and *An Outcast of the Islands.* These topics are now approached and represented, however, in radically different ways. Where he had earlier entangled discourse of race and gender in narrative of European and Malay cross-cultural encounters, the Mediterranean settings of his last three novels combine with a sharper focus on issues of gender. Recent criticism has revealed that what was once called Conrad's 'uncongenial subject' is, in fact, an area of subtle and complex analysis, and the historical and political material of his last fictions provides the basis for the throughgoing examination of masculinity that *Chance* and *Victory* begun."

3 Joseph Conard's Short Stories

Much of Conrad's time and energy went into the writing of short stories for magazines, since he badly needed the relatively high remuneration that this mode of writing provided. Short story is an elastic term in the Conrad canon, embracing pieces that range from short and slight tales to novellas as lengthy and important as *Heart of Darkness*. Nearly all were originally published in a great variety of British and American magazines. Conrad collected twenty-five of his stories in a series of six volumes, and a further four stories were collected in a posthumous volume.

Gail Fraser observes, "Although Conrad's fascination with the novel, as a form of art has been well documented by Ford Madox Ford and others, Conrad seldom used the term to refer to his own longer works. In their subtitles, he described six of his novels as 'tales' and one as a story,' thus emphasizing the older and larger category of narrative fiction. In his letters also, he preferred not to distinguish between short fiction and novels, referring to both forms as 'stories.' This blurring of generic boundaries reflects the organic evolution of may of his works. For example, *Nostromo,* which he was still calling a 'story' after writing 560 manuscript pages, actually began as a short story before it became a 'long short story', and then a 'long story' or 'novel.' Indeed, any overview of Conrad's creative process would reveal an essentially Darwinian approach to writing fiction in that his art forms are continually being modified by the pressures of their environment."

Gail Fraser thinks Conrad seems to have achieved his best work, regardless of length, by allowing the single episode to open up thematic and formal possibilities as he wrote. And it may well be that such artistic risk-taking demanded modest beginnings.

There may also be more than one reason why Conrad found the short form so appealing when he first though of an idea for a story. It had been successfully exploited by writers like

Maupassat, Flaubert, and Turgenev, whose craftsmanship he carefully studied and admired. Perhaps for this reason, almost from the beginning of his career as an author Conrad avoided the temptation to describe short fiction as a lesser art. Before his first volume of short stories appeared, he wrote to Fisher Unwin, his English publisher at the time, that the current 'slump' in the market was illogical, because 'the intrinsic value of a work can have nothing to do' with its length (Letters, II p. 49). In this respect he was, again, unlike Henry James, whose fondness for the *nouvelle* is well known but who emphasizes the limitations of the short from when describing the challenge or writing within a form 'that, at the best, would give little.'

The shorter forms of Conrad's fiction have yet another significance in the larger pattern of his writings, for they are part of an important alternating rhythm. "Typhoon" would be 'a fresh start' after the 'nightmare' of finishing *Lord Jim* (Letters, II, p. 289), and writing "The Secret Sharer" in the midst of *Under Western Eyes* gave him confidence.

When Conrad learned that "An Outpost of Progress," his first story to be published, would be printed in two instalments, he objected that its division would damage the cumulative effect of his ironic method: 'I told the unspeakable idiots that the thing halved would be as ineffective [sic] as a dead scorpion. There will be a part without the sting—and the part with the sting—and being separated they will be both harmless and disgusting' (Letters, I, p. 320). In this and later stories like "Amy Foster" and "The Secret Sharer," serial division into two or three parts destroyed the reader's sense of uninterrupted communion with the author and his work—a feature that helps to distinguish the genre. In this respect, Conrad would have agreed with most critics writing about short fiction today, who argue that the experience of reading a shorter work is different from that of reading a novel because of the way memory functions in relation to quantity and duration. Conrad was in fact arguing for the integrity of the modern short story as an art form. Conrad's failure to sell 'The Return' points to another limitation of magazine as opposed to book publication: the editorial concern to satisfy middle-class tastes.

"Falk," was never serialized– its hero confesses to cannibalism –and two more stories, "The Idiots" and "Freya of the Seven

Isles," were refused at least once, apparently because they made too little concession to market formulae: an inoffensive subject, simplicity of style or treatment, and a happy ending.

Conrad was proud of his literary talent as a short story writer and he said once: "My talent...appeals to such widely different personalities as W.H. [sic] Henley and Bernard Shaw—H.G. Wells and professor Yrgö Hirn of the Finland University—to Maurice Greiffenhagen a painter and to the skipper of a Persian Gulf steamer who wrote to the papers of my 'Typhoon'—to the Ed of PMM [*Pall Mall Magazine*] to a charming old lady in Winchester"(Letters, II, p. 416).

The pressures of serial publication on the form and style of Conrad's short fiction become most evident after Pinker's failure to place "Falk" and "Amy Foster" as quickly as he had hoped. Written after "Amy Foster" and as a companion-piece to it, "To-morrow" conforms much more readily to the standard pattern of magazine fiction.

Tales of Unrest (1898)

Conrad's first collection of short stories was published by Fisher Unwin, London in 1898 in an edition of 3000 copies. The dedication is to Adolf Krieger. The volume contains five stories. A short story could generate income more rapidly, and sometimes more gratifyingly, than a novel. "An Outpost of Progress," for instance, earned him fifty pounds, and "The Idiots" forty-two pounds, from magazine editors quite substantial sums at that time. Norman Sherry notes that 'though *Tales of Unrest* was praised many reviewers pointed to the depressing nature of the tales. However, at the beginning of 1899, Conrad was one of three writers (the others were Sidney Lee and Maurice Hewlett) awarded a prize by the weekly academy for outstanding work produced during the previous year and observed that it was Conrad's achievement to have brought the East to our very ... doors.'

"Karain: a Memory": This story had originally appeared in the famous *Blackwood's* Magazine in 1897. In his later "Author's Note" Conrad states: 'it was my first contribution to *Blackwood's* Magazine and . . . led to my personal acquaintance with Mr William Blackwood' (the magazine was later to publish "Youth,"

Heart of Darkness, and other works by Conrad). Like his first two novels, it has a Malayan setting and its protagonist is haunted by the ghost of a man he has killed. As Baines comments, it 'oozes lush romanticism.'

"The Idiots": This story was published in the *Savoy* in 1896. It was written during Conrad's honeymoon earlier in that year and was suggested by an actual encounter with children in Brittany. In a letter to Garnett it is described as 'a short story of Brittany Peasant life.' A lurid tale of murder and suicide, it nevertheless has a certain crude effectiveness, as well as being of some psychological interest in relation to Conrad's feelings about marriage and parenthood. It shows the influence of Maupassant.

"An Outpost of Progress": The best story in the collection. "An Outpost of Progress," appeared in *Cosmopolis* in 1897, having also been written during Conrad's 1896 honeymoon in Brittany. His letter to Garnett says that he is 'pleased with it'; and on the same day he wrote to Unwin, 'It is a story of the Congo. There is no love interest in it. . .. The 'Author's Note' describes it as 'the lightest part of the loot I carried off from Central Africa', and declares, 'it is true enough in its essentials.' Its relationship to the more substantial part of his African loot *Heart of Darkness*, is a significant one: like that slightly later story, though in balder terms, its concern is with the moral disintegration of Europeans in tropical Africa.

Kayerts and Carleir are promised quick profits as managers of a jungle trading station, the same fundamental situation as that of Almayer and, later, of Kurtz. Their compromise involves paradox in that they accept a life of hardship, isolation and savagery in expectation of eventual luxury and social elevation.

Sick and demoralized, the two men drift into a series of trivial personal disputes, in the last of which Kayerts mistakenly shoots and kills his companion. Before the body can be buried the company director returns with his steamer, and Kayerts hangs himself in fear and remorse. The catastrophe which concludes the story is a recognizable short version of the usual Conradian ending, in which a figure from the hero's former world arrives to pass judgment.

S.K. Land thinks this short story exhibits features of the structural pattern of *An Outcast of the Islands*.

"The Return": This story was written just after "Karain" in 1897. The "Author's Note" describes it as 'a left-handed production' and recalls how much it cost its author 'in sheer toil, in temper and in disillusion.' He was unable to place it with an editor. It is set not in Malaya or the Congo, but in 'fashionable London society,' and explores the nature of a marriage relationship.

"The Lagoon:" The last and shortest story in the volume had appeared in the top-drawer *Cornhill Magazine* in 1897, and was another product of the previous year's honeymoon. Set in Malaya, and described in a letter to Garnett as very much Malay indeed, it returns to the world of Conrad's first two novels. He himself makes this point in his "Author's Note": 'It . . . marks, in a manner of speaking, the end of my first phase.'

In this story an unnamed white man is paddled by Malays via a narrow approach to a lagoon where a Malay friend lives in seclusion with his wife. The latter is dying, and the Malay tells the story of how he carried off the girl and, in his flight, abandoned the brother who was helping him and who met his death at the hands of the pursuers. The wife dies, and the man will now go to seek revenge for his brother's death.

Though a slight story, "The Lagoon" contains some typical Conradian motifs. The Malay is an exile, living outside the world of action to which he can return only after the death of the woman for whose sake he has sacrificed his brother. His sudden, unpremeditated, irrevocable and bitterly regretted step in pushing off the boat and leaving his brother behind looks forward to Jim's jump from the *Patna*.

Youth: A Narrative and Two Other Stories (1902)

Conrad's second collection of stories was issued by the Edinburgh publishing firm of Blackwood's. The volume appeared in 1902 in an edition of 3150 copies. As Norman Sherry points out in *Critical Heritage*, reviewers tended to follow the lead of Edward Garnett who praised the collection. Garnett had referred to "Youth" as 'a modern English epic of the Sea' and had praised *Heart of Darkness* as 'the high-water mark of the author's talent.' The volume, which Conrad referred to as 'the three-headed monster in the green cover', was dedicated to his wife.

"Youth," subtitled *"A Narrative:"* It is also described as 'a feat of memory' and 'a record of experience.' The manuscript shows that Conrad had considered, and rejected, "A Voyage" as an alternative title. It is closely based on his own ill-fated first voyage to the East on the *Palestine* in 1881-3. More recently, Najder has extended Baines' argument by showing that there are at least two major discrepancies between Conrad's experience and the account given in "Youth." In the first place, "Conrad dramatized the accident, stretching it out in time and space and giving a different reason for parting with the towing steamer. In the tale the parting appears extremely risky; in reality, however, the disaster took place near shore. The boats did not steer for Java but toward the port of Muntok on Bangka island."

In other words, this is fictionalized autobiography, like so much of Conrad's work. The story is one of Conrad's best-known and, much antholog-ized and used as a school text. It must have contributed to the popular conception of him as primarily a teller of tales about the sea. Its telling, however, shows a degree of sophistication and it is important as introducing for the first time the figure of Marlow as narrator-participant. As in *Heart of Darkness* a little later, the story is set in a frame situation: a group of five men, 'a director of companies, an accountant, a lawyer, Marlow, and myself,' all sharing the strong bond of the sea, are sitting round a table after dinner; and to his fellow-diners Marlow tells 'the story, or rather the chronicle of a voyage.' Marlow, as a mature and reflective man of the sea, has much in common with Conrad (he even has the same number of letters); on the other hand, he is not Conrad and is seen objectively both by his creator and by the narrator of the frame-story. Conrad evidently liked the device so well that he revived it not only in *Heart of Darkness* but in *Lord Jim* and *Chance*; moreover, he developed the role of Marlow, so that the Marlow of, for example, *Lord Jim* performs a considerably more complex and subtle function than his namesake of "Youth." No doubt, Conrad was attracted by the opportunity of being able to comment and ruminate on the action without resorting to the intrusive interpolations of an omniscient narrator beloved by Thackeray, Trollope, and other Victorian novelists but distinctly out of favour by the turn of the century. The use of Marlow also enabled him to employ a more relaxed, informal, semi-colloquial style that may have acted as a corrective to the tendency to over-writing that had afflicted the lush prose of his earliest work.

In "Youth" Conrad not only drew on the events and feelings of his own past but used not for the first the names of actual men and an actual ship either thinly disguised or not disguised at all: the *Palestine* appears as the *Judea,* and the captain (Beard) and the mate (Mahon) both appear under their own names.

"The End of the Tether" : This story was begun in 1902, just after Conrad and Hueffer had completed their collaboration on Romance. Captain Whalley, the protagonist, has much in common with Michael Henchard in Hardy's *The Mayor of Casterbridge.* An older man with a daughter whom he loves dearly, he comes to grief partly through ill-luck (he loses his savings through a bank failure, and he begins to lose his sight) but also through yielding to temptation after an upright life (he becomes involved in some shady business dealings). The ensuing moral discovery—that 'All his spotless life had fallen into the abyss'—leads to his death. Unlike the other two stories in the volume, "The End of the Tether" uses the conventional third-person mode of narration. Perhaps for this reason an anonymous reviewer in the *Times Literary Supplement* thought it the best of the three, a view shared by Henry James, though not by later critics.

Blindness, however, is a symptom, not the moral root of Whalley's problem, which lies deeper and which precedes the onset of his disability. The Captain first commits himself to an anomalous situation when he enters into partnership with the uncongenial Massy, a venture about which he has serious doubts on account of Massy's character and because, in tacitly allowing his new partner to continue under the delusion that he was a wealthy man. Whalley has practised on him a small but deliberate deception.

The paradox of Whalley, the eminent explorer and sea-captain who cannot see, is a symptom and emblematic outgrowth of the bargain with Massy, which is in turn a classic instance of the ambivalent compromise of the Conradian hero. Whalley's taking command of the Sofala and associating himself with the disreputable Massy, particularly under a shadow of false pretense, gives the hero cause for thought.

Whalley's end is determined from the moment of the bargain which makes him Captain and shareholder of the steamer in which he will drown.

S. K. Land observes, "On the other hand, Whalley's motives, even more than those of Kurtz, Jim and Falk, are pure and worthy. He is, indeed, the most selfless and least culpable of Conrad's heroes to date. His object in associating with Massy is in no sense personal gain, for he wishes only to support himself while preserving his capital for his impoverished daughter." It is for this small grain of human pride that Whalley suffers.

***Typhoon and other Stories* (1902)**

"Typhoon": "Typhoon" was published in the *Pall Mall Magazine* in three instalments in 1902. It appears to have been written in 1901. In 1919 Conrad added an 'Author's Note' in which he states that the central incident is based on real life. The name of MacWhirr is borrowed from the captain under whom Conrad had served on the *Highland Forest*. The "Author's Note" also makes the important point that the real subject of the story is 'not the bad weather but the extraordinary complication brought into the ship's life at a moment of exceptional stress by the human element below her deck.' This story is actually treated as a novel and it is analyzed in the second chapter.

"Amy Foster": This story was serialized in the weekly *Illustrated London News* in 1901. Conrad may have appreciated the irony by which thestory of a community's lack of charity appeared over the Christmas period. It was written quite quickly in the same year, immediately after "Falk." The germ of the story seems to have been suggested by Hueffer, and it is not difficult to see that the simple but powerful situation of a shipwrecked man's failure to communicate with the ignorant folk among whom he found himself would make a strong personal appeal to Conrad. Personal tragedy, exile, linguistic isolation, and almost intolerable loneliness all conspire to make the protagonist's plight intensely pathetic.

A central European peasant, lured by false promises, decides to seek his fortune in America but is cast away and washed ashore near an English village. The villagers treat him brutally, regarding him as a drunken tramp; the only person who makes a gesture of kindness is the slow-witted servant Amy Foster, whom he at length marries. She is bewildered by his wish to teach their child his native language; and when he falls ill and in his delirium babbles in a strange tongue she abandons him and he dies alone. (Conrad himself was to revert to Polish in his final illness.)

Gail Fraser thinks "Like 'Typhoon', 'Amy Foster' and 'The Secret Sharer' show us how Conrad's best short fiction tends to emphasize mythic or universal paradigms of experience.

"To-morrow:" "To-morrow" published in the *Pall Mall Magazine* in 1902, is the only story in the collection that falls short of being a masterpiece. A couple of years later Conrad turned it into a one-act play and it was staged under the title *One Day More;* the dramatic version was published in 1919.

Captain Hagberd is an elderly widower of eccentric habits and on retiring from the sea has settled in the little seaport of Colebröok. His only son has long ago run away to sea, and thold man becomes obsessed with preparations for the return that he believes to be imminent. But the things go wrong.

"Falk:" "Falk" was written immediately after "Typhoon" and finished in 1901. Conrad later commented that it was 'partly biographi-cal being an episode in the story of my first command.' The subject of cannibalism made it unpalatable to editors. The episode has taken place 'many years ago ... in a certain Eastern seaport' when the story-teller was not thirty yet, and concerns a German skipper, Hermann, whose wife and children live with him on his ship and whose existence is bourgeois. Hermann toiled upon the seas much as a shopkeeper works behind his counter. The ship is named the *Diana* and is a most innocent old ship, and seemed to know nothing of the wicked sea, as there are on shore households that know nothing of the corrupt world.

"Falk" is a masterly narrative in Conrad's most accomplished ironic vein and has a very agreeably astringent humour. Baines points out that, while tone and treatment are quite different, "Falk" has something in common with *Heart of Darkness.* "Falk" belongs with *Typhoon,* not only chronologically but also as Conrad's only other major story in a predominantly comic mood.

Just as *Typhoon* portrays the success of a man who is in every significant way Jim's opposite, so in "Falk" we see a man who, like Jim, bears the guilt of a heinous but ambivalent sin, but who is able despite this to circumvent his rivals and win his lady. Falk is therefore a Conradian hero of much the same general type as Willems who seeks to overcome these disadvantages by making a new start in a new sphere.

The hero's move towards the world of the *Diana* is typically centered upon the heroine, Hermann's niece, who embodies much of her uncle's spirit. She is placid, domestically inclined, even tempered and modest, neat and apparently pure. At the same time, however, there is about her a power, size and vitality which clearly provide the basis of the attraction she holds for Falk. To Falk, Hermann's niece represents the ideal of vitalism. Later the worthy Hermann himself is cast as Falk's rival.

In the story of Falk Conrad also develops his favourite theme of reputation. The narrator's part in "Falk" resembles that of Marlow in *Heart of Darkness* with respect to the matter of the hero's reputation. The difference between Marlow in *Heart of Darkness* and the narrator in "Falk" is that the former is also the hero's nemesis while the latter is the instrument of his release and rehabilitation.

There is an interesting recent discussion of "Falk" in Tony Tanner's essay "Gnawed Bones" and "Artless Tales"—Eating and Narrative in Conrad', in *Joseph Conrad: A Commemoration* ed Norman Sherry (1976).

A Set of Six (1908)

Each of the six stories in this volume carries a categorizing subtitle, and all had been previously published in magazines in 1906. The book was published by Methuen of London in 1908 in an edition of 1500 copies; the American edition did not appear until 1915. *Critical Heritage* reprints an interesting selection of reviews together with Conrad's deeply felt responses to them. W.L. Courtney declared that 'two, or perhaps, three of the stories are masterpieces, while all of them stand at an exceedingly high level of workmanship and literary value.'

"Caspar Ruiz: A Romantic Tale": This was serialized in the *Pall Mall Magazine* in 1906. It is set in Chile and seems to have been begun late in 1904, shortly after the completion of Conrad's South American novel, Nostromo, and finished in 1905. The hero is a

giant of a man who escapes a firing-squad, becomes a fugitive, and leads a band of rebels; in a siege he offers his body as a gun-carriage, but his back is broken. Beginning as a third-person narrative, it quickly turns into the reminiscences of an old man recalling his youth. Robert Lynd thought it 'worth all the rest of the book' and said that Conrad had written 'a story to compare with [Turgenev's] "A Lear of the Steppes." In 1920 Conrad collaborated with Pinker on a film script based on this story and titled *Caspar-the Strung Man*.

"The Informer: An Ironic Tale": This appeared in *Harper's Magazine* in 1906. It reads like an offshoot of *The Secret Agent*, a version of which had been completed and serialized by 1906: the story deals with anarchists in London, the character of the Professor is briefly sketched, and the comment that 'anarchists, I suppose, have no families' hints ironically at Mr Verloc.

"The Brute: an Indignant Tale": This concerns a ship that has the reputation of causing men's deaths and finally runs aground because the officer of the watch is occupied with a woman. There is an intentional ambiguity in the opening, where 'she' appears to refer to a woman but actually designates the ship. Again, a first-person frame-narrative accommodates the narrative of another speaker. Original publication was in the *Daily Chronicle* in 1906. Baines calls it 'little more than a pot-boiler.'

"An Anarchist: A Desperate Tale": This was completed in 1905 and appeared in *Harper's Magazine* in 1906. Set on a South American cattle estate, it shows that a little thing may bring about the undoing of a man. The first-person narrator, a lepidopterist, tells how a decent French workman has been caught in the toils of anarchists and is now virtually the slave of a great capitalist enterprise.

"The Duel: A Military Tale": It was serialized in the Pall Mall Magazine in 1908. The longest of the stories in this volume, it is set at the time of the Napoleonic Wars. Its third-person narrative relates how a quarrel begins over a triviality and continues through many years against a background of war and politics. Garnett praised it as 'a masterpiece of style' and 'in the unerring delicacy of its artistic strokes. . . worthy of Turgeney.'

An inoffensive but unremarkable soldier, he is drawn into a pointless quarrel with a fellow officer which, through no fault of his, becomes a lasting and widely-known feud. He wishes only to forget the affair, but is allowed no honourable way of doing so. Unlike the Count, however, d'Hubert finally faces and defeats his antagonist, a victory which also brings him the love of his heroine.

"Il Conde: A Pathetic Tale": This was published in *Cassell's Magazine* in 1908. An old gentleman of hypersensitive nature is robbed and threatened in Naples, with devastating effect upon his personality. The first-person narrative incorporates the victim's own account of the incident.

The story is about an elderly gentlemen who has enjoyed a completely calm, private and untroubled life. When suddenly forced to confront violence and lawlessness from a member of his own social class, he is shattered by the shock and goes into decline.

'Twixt Land and Sea (1912)

The volume contains three stories, all previously published, and appeared in London and New York in 1912. The English publisher Dent printed 3500 copies. The critical reception was in general very favourable: the *Times Literary Supplement*, for instance, proclaimed the three stories 'each a masterpiece.'

"A Smile of Fortune": This story was first appeared in the *London Magazine* in February 1911. Subtitled "Harbour Story," it is the least satisfac-tory of the three stories. The narrator is the captain of a ship that visits a tropical island referred to as the 'Pearl of the Ocean' in order to collect a cargo of sugar. There he meets a ship's chandler, Jacobus, visits the latter's home, and is powerfully attracted to his daughter Alice, a wild, surly girl who is the illegitimate offspring of Jacobus's infatuation with a circus artiste. The girl is described in strongly physical, even erotic terms, and there appears to be a suggestion of symbolism in her setting, a beautiful garden in which she passes her days almost as a recluse. The captain falls in love with her, but after delays in getting the cargo aboard the time comes for him to leave the island, and he does so without committing himself to her. To ease his conscience he spends every penny he possesses on buying a load of potatoes from her father as an investment- an act that at first seems ludicrous but that turns out to be 'a smile of fortune' when he arrives in a colony where the potato harvest has failed

and he is able to dispose of the potatoes at a handsome profit. Like "The Secret Sharer" in the same volume, the story concerns a young captain's initiation through experience into a knowledge of the world. The third story in the volume, "Freya of the Seven Isles," presents a heroine who has something in common with the Alice of the story.

According to Baines, certain elements in "A Smile of Fortune" were drawn from Conrad's visit to Mauritius with his first command of the *Otago*. The story is one of Conrad's best and has provoked extensive commentary. Albert Guerard's psycho-analytical interpretation sees Leggatt as a 'lowerself of the captain.'

"The Secret Sharer": "The Secret Sharer" presents the most explicit expression of the theme which Conrad had already developed in *Heart of Darkness* and *Lord Jim:* the underlying kinship between all men—saint and sinner, Marlow and Kurtz, Jim and Gentleman Brown. The actual name of the story as well as some alternates suggested by Conrad are "The Second Self," "The Secret Self," and "The Other Self."

The story concerns a young and inexperienced sea captain; who, taking the anchor watch one night, sees a man in the water clinging to a rope ladder lowered over the side of the ship. When the Captain brings the man on board he learns that the stranger, named Leggatt, has just escaped from a nearby ship the *Sephora* where shortly before in a storm at sea, he, the First Mate, had killed a disobedient member of the crew. Almost at once the Captain notices a "mysterious communication . . . already established between us two," while Leggatt observes that the Captain act" 'as if you had expected me.' The Captain says, "It was, in the night, as though I had been faced by my own reflection in the depths of a sombre and immense mirror.' The Captain hides the fugitive Leggatt in his cabin.

The Captain experiences a curious disturbance in his sense of identity—an alienation from himself. When he is temporarily separated from Leggatt it seems as if "part of me is absent." His mind is affected, he believes, for he has become unsure of himself, neglecting to give orders which had always been second nature to him. Finally, after several days at sea, he selects a spot where Leggatt can safely disembark; the Captain brings his ship perilously close to the shore and his "double" secretly lowers himself into the water and quietly swims to the land, to become, like Jim, "a fugitive and a vagabond on the earth."

There is indeed a dreamlike quality to the nocturnal happenings in "The Secret Sharer," recalling Marlow's comment to his audience in *Heart of Darkness*, for the language of "The Secret Sharer," the strangeness of its story, and the eerie atmosphere that pervades it conspire to recreate what Marlow calls "the dream sensation, that commingling of absurdity, surprise, and bewilderment in a tremor of revolt, that notion of being captured by the incredible."

"The Secret Sharer" has been the target of more many-sided interpretations than any other Conrad work with the possible exception of *Heart of Darkness*. The story deals with the theme of apprenticeship-to-life. The work has the psychological phenomenon of the alter ego. The Captain is like the fugitive Leggatt. The use of ideas like doubles, second self, secret self, other self evidence this. Frederick Karl observes, 'The Secret Sharer' is the other side of *Under Western Eyes*: the Captain is a Razumov who does not betray his trust, and Leggatt is a Haldin who escapes his oppressors. The two works taken together pose a double question and show the consequences leading from both answers: what happens when you betray a trust? and what happens when under duress you remain true to your secret? It is the Captain's recognition of these points that sustains the dramatic interest of the story."

Professor Zabel, in his well-known essay "Joseph Conrad: Chance and Recognition," remarked that the crisis in every one of Conrad's novels and stories arrives when by accident, decision, or error a man finds himself abruptly committed to his destiny. This recognition, Zabel says, occurs through a series of steps: isolation of the character from society; his recognition of his situation in a hostile world; and then, once self-knowledge is attained, his way, as we saw with Razumov, of either solving or succumbing to his problem. This is also the problem of the artist; and Conrad through his particular way of developing "The Secret Sharer" was able to relate the psychological and moral contradictions in human nature to the ambivalence of reality as art embodies it, and finally to a searching analysis of value itself.

Commensurate with this search for value in life, another way of looking at *Heart of Darkness* suggests itself (with "The Secret Sharer" also in mind): the journey of Marlow-Conrad into the Congo is a means to self-knowledge in which the crucial experience is a process of maturation into both adulthood and artistry; once the journey into this turmoil of experience has been resolved, the survivor is able to proceed to live and create. The experiences of Marlow-Conrad in the Congo, together with the Captain's experience on his ship, are forms of initiation which all must undergo, but which only the true artist in life or fiction can successfully sustain. This story, then, becomes a microcosm of Conrad's major themes; but for all its suggestiveness, it is, paradoxically, one of his most straightforward and obvious works. Its narrative is a model of clarity, like those uncomplicated narratives "Youth" and *The Shadow Line* (1917).

Royal Gettmann observes, The Secret Sharer is of a class of stories all too rare. It has, as so many modern stories do not, a sustained and combined appeal. It offers the immediate appeal of an action or adventure story as well as the aesthetic pleasures of symbolic, psychological, and moral investigation."

Conrad's depiction of Leggat is the captain's hiden self, his alter ego.

In the final analysis, Conrad's greatest interest is in the moral aspect of the story. When the Captain states the theme early in the story, saying "I wondered how far I should turn out faithful to that ideal conception of one's own personality every man sets up for himself secretly," he is talking about more than psychology: he is worried about his moral state.

Within the Tides (1915)

The volume, published in 1915 in an edition of 3,500 copies, brings together four stories published between 1911 and 1914 and adds an interesting "Author's Note."

"The Planter of Malata": This was written in 1913 and originally titled "The Assistant." It appeared in a New York periodical the *Metropolitan Magazine* in 1914 Felicia Moorson, the daughter of a famous scientist and philosopher, has been engaged to a man Arthur in England, but when he is accused of embezzlement she

has believed in his guilt and he has left the country. Subsequently she receives proof that he is innocent, and, accompanied by her father and an aunt, sets out to seek him in order to set matters right by marrying him. Her search brings her at length to a great colonial city in the Antipodes (presumably Sydney), where she meets Geoffrey Renouard, who is running a silk farm on a nearby island. He falls passionately in love with her, but eventually realizes that the man she is seeking is his own former assistant, who has recently died. In order to prevent her from going away, he tells her that the man is on the island but says nothing of his death. She goes to the island, where he tells her about the man's grave and tells her of his own love. She refuses him, and departs; and Renouard commits suicide by setting out to swim beyond the confines of life—his eyes fixed on a star. This incurable romanticism makes him a blood-brother of such Conradian heroes as Lord Jim; ironically enough, the woman who rejects him is made of the same stuff, her unfulfilled mission being no more than a quixotic gesture. The story's central situation has power, but its infatuated hero does not entirely carry conviction. Baines points out that in its extreme romanticism it has something in common with "Freya of the Seven Isles."

The Planter of Malata is more serious piece and forms a closer parallel to Victory, with which it was contemporaneous. The hero, Renouard, is a paler version of Heyst, a man who chooses to withdraw from the corruption and superficiality of society to a virtually solitary life on a small island.

S.K. Land observes, "The paradox of the story is woven across a dualism which is, once again, recognizably similar to that of *Victory*. Renouard, like Heyst, oscillates between the poles of rejection of worldly values and involvement in human affairs. In this story the heroine herself symbolizes the world, whereas Lena in *Victory* is one of its victims; the paradoxical nature of Renounard's personality is shown simply in his selection of Felicia as the embodiment of his ideal. The two of them, hero and heroine, themselves stand for mutually repellent poles: the fallen world and its rejection, high society and 'plebeian' industry (p. 75), Felicia's theatrical idea of self-sacrifice and Remouard's consuming love."

"The Partner": This appeared in *Harper's Magazine* in November 1911. It concerns the wrecking of a ship in order to obtain the insurance money, and is not unfairly dismissed by Baines as 'an obvious pot-boiler'.

"The Inn of the Two Witches": This appeared in the *Pall Mall Magazine* in 1913 and in the New York *Metropolitan Magazine* in 1913, having been written towards the end of 1912. It is a retelling of a gothic tale. Set in Spain during the Peninsular War, it tells how a British naval officer goes in search of a sailor who has been sent on a mission and has disappeared. In a lonely inn he discovers the sailor's body and narrowly escapes sharing his fate: he has been suffocated by a four-poster bed with a top that can be lowered by a mechanism operated in the next room, this crime having been regularly perpetrated by the avaricious and witch-like women who keep the inn. There is genuine horror in the scene in which the officer discovers the sailor's corpse.

"Because of the Dollars": It appeared until the title "Lauching Anne" in the *Metropolitan Magazine* (New York) in 1914 having been written at the end of 1913. Under its earlier title it was dramatized by Conrad in 1921. Set in the Malay Archipelago, it tells how Captain Davidson, who is carrying a cargo of dollars, is plotted against by a group of villains. They plan to murder him and steal the money, but he is warned by a wretched woman Ann on whom he has taken pity and they are foiled. The woman is killed as an act of revenge by the ringleader of the plotters; Davidson, feeling acute remorse, adopts her son and is recompensed for his charitable deed by incurring the suspicion of his mean-spirited wife, who believes the child to be his own. So his wife returns to her family in Europe. The character Bamtz helps Davidson. Davidson befriends Laughing Ann who is then, in a roundabout way, killed in helping to save him from bandits. When he takes responsibility for her orphaned child his unsympathetic wife refuses to believe his explanation of the infant, assumes it to be his own, and makes this her excuse for returning to her family in Europe.

Although superficially a tale of villainy outwitted, therefore, it ends on a serious and even pessimistic note. Davidson's name suggests that he may conceivably be seen as a Christ-figure, with the woman as a Magdalene. This character Davidson is also seen in Conrad's novel Victory. But his role is dominant in the short story.

Tales of Hearsay (1925)

Conrad's seventh and last collection of stories was published posthumously in 1925, with a preface by R.B. Cunninghamc Graham, and brings together four stories, all published a number of years earlier in magazines: "The Warrior's Soul" (*Land and Water,* 1917), "Prince Roman" (*Oxford & Cambridge Review,* 1911, and *Metropolitan Magazine,* January 1912), "The Tale" (*Strand Magazine,* 1917), and "The Black Mate" (*London Magazine,* 1908). Richard Curie gave the volume its title.

"The Warrior's Soul": It was written in 1916 and, with "The Tale," seems to have been Conrad's only production during that barren and anxious year. It is a wartime story but set a hundred years back in the Napoleonic period which Conrad, like his contemporary Hardy, found so fascinating, and to which he was to turn again in his last novel *The Rover,* a few years later, as well as in his unfinished novel *Suspense.*

"Prince Roman": This was written somewhat earlier, towards the end of 1910, and at about the same time as "A Smile of Fortune." Its source is in Conrad's early years in Poland - partly on his meeting, during his childhood, with a certain Prince Roman Sanguszko, and partly on the memoirs of his Uncle Tadeusz published in 1900—and it seems to have been originally intended to form part of an autobiographical work.

"The Tale": Finished in 1916, it is a story of the Great War and hence related, and complementary, to "The Warrior's Soul." It also bears, as Baines has pointed out, a significant relationship to Conrad's short novel *The Shadow-Line,* written in the previous year, the story being 'almost an exact antithesis' to the novel in its moral theme.

"The Black Mate": The last story in the volume, "The Black Mate", is perhaps the most puzzling item in all Conrad's work. In 1886 Conrad seems to have submitted a story with this title for a competition in the popular British magazine *Tit-Bits;* his entry

was unsuccessful, and the story seems to have been lost. Yet Conrad's story of the name appeared once again. Jessie Conrad denied that there was any connection between the two stories; she insisted that she had given Conrad the idea for the 1908 story, and according to her version the two stories had only a title in common. The surviving story is a slight and light-hearted anecdote.

4 Joseph Conard and Worldview

Conrad and Poland (Russia), Imperialism, Modernism, Gothicism, the Problem of Language; Conrad and Great Writers: Schopenhauer, Nietzsche, Rousseau; John Galsworthy, R. B. Cunninghame Graham and Ford Madox Ford; Dickens and Hardy; and Conrad's Vision of life.

Conrad and Poland **(Russia)**

Joseph Conrad was a Pole, having been born in Berdyzow, then under the Russian rule. His father was a nobleman. His relatives the Bobrowskis were well off. In fact, his uncle Thaddeus Bobrowski who brought him up lived there. Conrad visited Poland often.

Norman Sherry writes, "Certainly Thaddeus had tried in vain to secure Conrad Austrian citizenship, but just as certainly the question why Conrad left his homeland cannot be fully answered. Years later, in *A Personal Record*, Conrad raised that mysterious question. 'Why should I...undertake the pursuit of fantastic meals of salt junk and hard tack upon the wide seas? ...The part of the inexplicable should be allowed for in appraising the conduct of men in a world where no explanation is final.' In any case, in October 1874, Conrad left Poland for Marseilles, with introductions arranged and a reasonable amount of money 2,000 francs a year in monthly instalments. Behind him already was more tragic experience than is given to many men in a lifetime: he was moved by the unlikely impulse, for a native of a land-locked country, to become a seaman; and, not yet seventeen, he was stepping alone into a new existence. This action, in its essentials, was to become a characteristic one of Conrad at intervals during his life."

Conrad had other relations in Poland. He liked his cousin Madame Poradowska who was a beautiful woman and writer.

Conrad's wife later wrote that 'she was, I think, the most beautiful woman I have ever seen.' She was the statuesque, forceful kind of woman to whom Conrad seems to have been always attracted.

The Conrads visited Poland in 1914. The First World War had begun then. They took refuge with a relative who had a house in the Carpathians, but in early October Conrad decided they must try to get home. They stayed in Vienna five days, since Conrad had gout. From Milan he cabled Pinker for money. They reached England on 3 November. Jessie commented, 'We had a narrow escape.'

It is now very widely accepted that Conrad's profound concern with problems of moral failure, of desertion, of betrayal, in a large part sprang from guilt feeling about his own abandonment of Poland–a Poland helpless under an alien tyranny. When at sixteen, the argument runs, he went off to France and the sea, he was taking the first step, no doubt unconsciously, towards the abandonment of the land for which his ancestors, indeed his own parents had suffered. That abandonment was made absolute eleven years later when he became a British citizen. And it was the sense of guilt implanted by this act that was the inspiration of much of his writing, and most clearly of all, *Lord Jim*. Jim's fatal jump to safety echoed the young Korzeniowski's flight from Poland.

Conrad was indeed a Pole, but it is too often forgotten that he was also a Russian citizen, a subject of the two successive Alexanders II and III. As a subject of the Tsar he was liable for conscription into the Imperial Army. What he renounced in 1886 was Russian, not Polish, citizenship. His own country did not exist: it was partitioned between the three monarchies, Russia, Prussia and Austria. Conrad transferred his formal allegiance from the dully reactionary Alexander III to Queen Victoria during the third administration of Mr. Gladstone.

In 1890 Conrad met his uncle Thaddeus in Kiev. The latter gave him the so called "Document." He said he spent 3,600 + 17,454 rubles for Conrad's upbringing. The uncle opposed Conrad's wish to go to Congo.

This is how Conrad writes of his motherland and his mother tongue. In fact, he spoke in Polish often.

Conrad and Imperialism

Terry Eagleton thinks the arguments range widely, in fact, from those who view Conrad as committed to a conservative, 'English view' of imperialism to those who see him as special to the whole enterprise and a champion of anti-colonial revolts. The Nigerian novelist Chinua Achebe's accusation that Conrad was 'a bloody racist' is countered by the contention of Ezekiel Mphahlele, a South African writer, that Conrad was one of the few 'outstanding white novelists who portray competently characters belonging to cultural groups outside their own.' D.C.R.A. Goonetilleke, writing from Sri Lanka, places Conrad with 'a distinguished minority of radical contemporary critics of imperialism such as Mark Twain, Roger Casement and E.D. Morel.' For some readers, then Conrad's works represent his time's dominant congratulatory imperial discourse: for others they subvert it. While many have agreed that in any case, the psychology of the colonialist most engages Conrad's attention, others contend that very backgrounding of native peoples and landscapes is objectionable.

"When I grow up I shall go there,' the eleven-year-old Jozef Teodor Konrad Korzeniowski promised himself, *'there* being the region of Stanely Falls which in 1868 was the blankest of blank spaces on the earth's figured surface. Although he would complain that geography was an under valued subject in Polish schools, such map-gazing must not have been an uncommon pursuit for mid-century Europeans stirred by the myriad reports of adventure and exploration filtering back to metropolitan centres from the colonial outposts of Africa, Asia and the Pacific.

By the time Conrad began working in the British Merchant Service in 1878, ten years after his childish boast, European imperial rule over the non-European world extended to nearly two-thirds of the Earth's land surface, and Britain's empire accounted for much of those holdings.

Another answer lies in the shifting nature of European imperialism itself between 1880 and 1914, a period during which colonial conquests accelerated worldwide. This 'new imperialism,' a complex response to the industrialized countries' growing needs and desires for food, raw materials, markets and investment opportunities, was pursued by such newcomers as

Germany, Belgium, Italy, the United States, and Japan, while Britain–which had been accumulating colonies for over two hundred years–and France redoubled their efforts. This multiplication of colonial powers seeking claims on ever-dwindling space, especially in the tropics, intensified rivalry. In Africa alone, European holdings climbed from eleven percent in 1875 to ninety per cent by 1902.

This period chronicles an external shift in the nature of imperialism itself and marks crucial developments in Corad's experience and outlook. He started to see colonialism closer up. From 1891, when he spent months in a London hospital recovering form his experience in the Congo, to 1895 and the publication of *Almayer's Folly,* Conrad was in England as much as he was at sea.

Europeans generally based their claims to rule primitive people on the basis of their own superiority, both technological and moral, and the English were no exception. 'The white man must rule,' Lord Milner told the Municipal Congress in Johannesburg in 1903 'because he is elevated by many, many steps above the black man.' Rudyard Kipling reiterated the same when he said that "East is east and west is west.'

Such arguments depicted continued expansion and control as not only moral and practical but somehow natural. Conrad's fiction, on the other hand, show the European intrusion as 'fantastic,' often criticizing it.

Andrea White in his essay "Conrad and Imperialism," observes, "Conrad's first two novels–*Almayer's Folly* and *An Outcast of the Islands—The Rescue,* many of his early stories, *Lord Jim* and *Victory,* depict the complex and competing racial and cultural relationships of native Dyaks, immigrant Chinese, Malay sultans, Arab rajahs and Dutch and English traders."

What Robert Louis Stevenson had also described in his South Seas fiction and J. A. Hobson later observed in his critique of Empire, *Imperialism* (1902), Conrad had seen for himself: that 'Greater Britain furnishes as convenient limbo for damaged characters and careers,' rather than emissaries of light going forth on the civilizing mission. Goonetilleke notes the correspondence between Conrad's and Hobson's thinking in this respect of *Victory,* but the observation holds true for Conrad's scepticism about the imperial venture generally and about the accompanying 'fine words' in particular, in its refusal to depict the Europeans in Sambir. Almayer himself is a bitter, failed Dutchman whose dreams of gold and glory in this backwater outpost have come to nothing. Lingrad, an English trader who 'invaded the Malay Archipelago in search of money and adventure,' becomes increasingly insubstantial and shadowy, and his flimsy hopes fail.

Conrad's fiction not only fail to privilege the Europeans appropriately, but represents the native point of view toward them, a view that does not distinguish one hated white man from another. While the natives call Lingard 'Rajah Laut' (King of the Sea), we are also given their less admiring view—that white men are duplicitous and destructive opportunists who have arrived with prayers on their lips and loaded guns in their hands. While Conrad's depiction of the white man in the tropics is subversively unheroic, his representation of the native also works to destabilize the hegemonic versions of the imperial endeavour. Babalatchi, for example, is indefatigable; we do not recognize him as belonging to a race of low efficiency.

Andrea White writes, "Conrad had already written three novels and five stories set in the Eastern seas, when in 1898 he sketched a beginning to *Lord Jim.* A more antithetical tale to the discourse of European supremacy could not have been told. The story of the actual *Jeddah,* a ship that carried Muslim pilgrims from Singapore to Jeddah was abandoned in stormy seas by her European officers in August 1880, must have deeply troubled those whose ideas of empire had been shaped by such public pronouncements as Chamberlain's and Salisbury's, that native people were backward brutes needing the more enlightened help of European civilizers."

In *Nostromo,* which Conrad first thought of in 1898 as a prospective story, he turns to a different kind of imperialism. While Costaguana is an independent country, it is an economic colony, and its leadership made up of Blanco families, the remaining Spanish élite, who, in turn, depend on foreign investment. The intervention of English and American money enables the silver from Chalres Gould's San Tomé mine to flow out, enriching foreign investors and Costaguana's Blanco families. Today's we recognize this situation as 'economic imperialism.'

Conrad knew that Amercian invention was as mischievous, as imperialistically motivated, as destructive as any of Europe's various incursions, partitioning, and annexations in Africa and Asia, or as Russia's in Poland. His fiction was instructive to colonized peoples, making them conscious in a new way of what it meant, exactly, to be colonized and to live in the glass cage of an imposed worldview, the first task in any project that undertakes the decolonization of the mind. The Guyanese novelist Wilson Harris speaks of the liberating effects of Conrad's fiction on his own writing which is also apparent in other post-Conradian legacies such as Jean Toomers's novel *Cane* (1923) and Wole Soyinka's play *The Road* (1973).

While Conrad's fiction inevitably bears traces of pervasive contemporary attitudes toward empire, and reveals his own anxiety, it contributes to revaluation of imperialism. For example, his *Heart of Darkness* exposed the machinery behind the apparent naturalness and inevitability of the imperial endeavour and made visible the conqueror's face hidden behind the mask of a civilizing mission's protestations of benevolence.

Conrad and Modernism

Kenneth Graham observes, "If we take Modernism to mean certain fundamental and more or less shared characteristics of those writers, thinkers, and artists of the period 1900-30, in Britain, Europe, America, and elsewhere, who are now (subjectively and from our own stance in history) seen as the most 'new' or responsive or influential of that time, it seems inevitable that Conrad should figure in that grouping."

Conrad's life and literary creations span the modernism age 1890 to 1930. Great Modernist works like Freud's *Interpretations of Dreams* (1900), Einstein's theories about relativity (1905), William James's *Pragmatism* (1912), Jung's *Psychology of the Unconscious* (1912), Picasso's *Les Demoiselles d'Avignon,* cubism came into vogue. Schonberg's musical compositions, Proust's *A la reacherche du tempts perdu* (1913), Mann's *Death in Venice* (1912), Gide's *Les Caves du Vatican* (1914), Rilke's *New Poems* (1907), Kafka's *Metamorphosis* (1915), Woolf's *The Voyage Out* (1915), Dorothy Richardson's Pointed Roofs (1915), Lawrence's *The Rainbow* (1914), Frazer's *The Golden Bough* (1914), Eliot's *"The*

Prufrock" Joyce's A Portrait, Yeats' *The Wild Swans* (1917), Forester's *A Passge to India* (1924) and of course Eliot's *The Waste Land* (1922) appeared.

Interestingly Conrad's major works *Heart of Darkness* (1899), *Under the Western Eye* (1911), *Victory* (1915), *The Shadow Lines* (1917), "The Secret Sharer" (1912), *Chance* (1914) appeared exactly in the period of modernism.

Conrad's one famous letter compares the universe to an impersonal machine: "It knits us in and it knits us out. It has knitted time space, pain, death, corruption, despair and all the illusions—and nothing matters" (Letters, I, p. 425). And in another letter: 'Faith is a myth and beliefs shift like mists on the shore; thoughts vanish; words, once pronounced, die; and the memory of yesterday is as shadowy as the hope of to-morrow.' Conrad's reductiveness may echo Hardy and Woolf; but it is as bleakly powerful and as annunciatory for the age to come as Mrs Moore's encounter with the emptiness of the absolute in Forster's Marabar Caves in *A Passage to India*, or Quentin Compson's final vision of sawdust-filled figures trapped in the ticking of a watch in Faulkner's *The Sound and the Fury* (1929).

The main similarity to the sensibility and ideas of the 1890s lies in Conrad's frequent rhetorical invocation of mystery and the unutterable, his glorification of the lonely artist (as in the Preface to *The Nigger of the 'Narcissus'*), and perhaps above all in his insertion of episodes of dream like experience, of hallucination, the effects of sudden loss of practical will, the sense of the world's reality falling away, into almost all his narratives of practical action and search—the disorienting effects of the river's fog on Marlow in *Heart of Darkness*, the evocation of the paralyzing darkeness in the Isabels episode of *Nostromo* and throughout *The Shadow-Line*, Razumov's long entrapment amid the phantasmagoria and unreal voices of the Chateau Borel, and Heyst's doomed brooding and inertia on Samburan.

It is said that *Heart of Darkness* calls for some further consideration as a Modernist manifesto, announcing in 1899 the note of its new era. The tale in its very essence concerns the unspoken, the buried side of human nature, with Kurtz as Marlow's unacknowledged other self- at the very outset of what may have seen as essentially the Freudian age. Freud's writings themselves, from *Studies in Hysteria* (1895) and *The Interpretation of Dreams* (1900) through *Totem and Taboo* (1912-13) and *Civilization and its Discontents* (1920), had a very mixed reactions from writers like Joyce and Woolf, a hostile reaction from Lawrance, and overtly none at all from Conrad. But the development of stream of consciousness by the first two of these writers as an expressive technique in narration could hardly have been possible without the revolutionary impact of Freudian concepts of the unconscious and the role of free association in the working of consciousness.

Heart of Darkness, characteristically, is not simply about Marlow's pursuit of his double, his shadow self, in neo-Freudian or even Jungian terms (a theme repeated intermittently throughout Conrad's work, through 'The Secret Sharer' and Victory down to *The Shadow-Line),* but is specifically modernist in that its technique as a narrative directly reflects its descent into the disorienting world of a new psychology.

All the pressures behind a generation poised on the edge flow into this inner strain and duplicity of Conrad's creative mind. It was an era obsessed, both liberatingly and despairingly, by the sense of its own fragmentation: the break-up of old structures, old conventions of art and thought and politics, with individual personality itself dissolving like a mirror held up to a mirror, or else revealing unconscious strata that could drive, abstract, or transform the self. It was an age of extremism, and it was an age of war, of 'the War to end all Wars.' Possessed by irony, these duplicitous writers of their time turned to extreme forms of experimentation to express their two-edged (and therefore Conradian) view of order: they express what Frank Kermode calls in 'the great experimental novels of early Modernism–Kafka, Proust, Joyce, Musil...a l 'nd of formal desperation.' And only some such oxymoron as formal desperation like the virtual oxymoron of truth or evil, like the hidden oxymoron of heart and darkness, is adequate to suggest the self-vexing dynamism and power of the Conradian enigma: which in its essence was the enigma, and even the driving force of Modernism itself.

Joseph Conrad and the Gothic

Joseph Conrad is writer of the best known novel Heart of Darkness. It is surprising to find Conrad employing such traditional Gothic techniques to create an atmosphere of imminent terror. However a short story like "The Inn of the Two Witches" (1915) provides a clear revelation of Conrad's acquaintance with and understanding of Gothicism in its most basic form. In this tale Conrad charts the story of Edgar Byrne and his search for young seaman, Tom Corbin, who has disappeared in mysterious circumstance. Significantly setting his action in a remote region of the early nineteenth century Spain, Conrad readily adopts a number of Gothic conventions aimed at creating a mood of initial terror. A sense of brooding oppression is achieved by his references to the "wild, gloomy sky" and the "rank," "stony" and dreary" "nature of the surrounding landscape." Edgar Byrne's search intensifies the Gothic atmosphere correspondingly. Stumbling on a remote hamlet, Conrad's narrative notes that it is "hidden in a fold in the ground," in spot which "seemed the most lonely corner of the earth and as if accursed in its uninhabited barrenness." In such passages Conrad's language, with its heavy adjectival stress, is ideally suited to the Gothic form, which by definition demands linguistic intensification. Michael Joslin observes, "In characteristic Gothic fashion," Conrad's landscape has become "a Grotesque vision of hell."

Conrad's opening narrative sequence in "The Inn of the Two Witches" (1915) follows well-established Gothic formulas designed to create a mood of initial error. In *Heart of Darkness* (1899), for example, one critic refers to the "powerful impact of the setting" with its "aura of nightmarish ...gloom" and adds significantly that its effect, according to Ian Watt, is as "startling as any created in a recognized Gothic novel. Conrad's stress on the reverberating darkness, the almost evil animation of the trees, is strikingly Gothic in its whole conception. Furthermore in this passage, it is significant to point to what Watt calls Conrad's characteristic "inflation of language." His lavish imagery so typical in his descriptions of Africa and the tropics creates an immediate sense of apprehension, and plays a major role in evoking a mood of fear and terror. 'Conrad's Sea' becomes as strangely mysterious and as powerfully moving as the awesome castles and the sublime mountains of the conventional terror novel.

Heart of Darkness is a narrative, with other two stories. The story begins with a western character Marlow meeting at the trading post and the central stations are only in extracting ivory and do not notice the suffering of the native workers. Marlow is sent upriver to rescue Kurtz, an agent, now seriously ill. His depravity is signaled by the human heads which decorate the posts outside the hut. Marlow retains a paradoxical admiration for Kurtz, whose deathbed cry—The horror! The Horror!—intimates a kind of desperate self knowledge.

Conrad's Problem of Language

Conrad learnt English at his age of 21. When he came to England he could not speak in good English. His one friend Hope said he spoke broken English. John Galsworthy said: "He spoke to me with a strong foreign accent. He seemed to me strange on an English ship." Jessie Conrad could not understand his English sometimes. His first English letter was to a Polish friend Spiridion Kliszczewski.

Still Conrad learnt English very fast. He said he learnt it by reading. Already he had mastered Polish, Russian and French. As we see his knowledge of the English and European literature, he read avidly. Conrad's equipment was remarkable. He was a good linguist, exceptionally well read in French and English literature. Knowing Poland and Russia from within, by temperament and heredity he was, as he told Mr. Megroz, 'Western European, descending from the Roman Empire and the ancient western world'. Well as he knew French, he recorded to the same author that he always thought in English, a remark he reinforces in *A Personal Record* by the conclusive sentence,' If I had not written in English I would not have written at all. "He took to letters an experience which was exceptional in its range, and an outlook wholly individual. He was shy of 'isms'—internationalism, cosmopolitanism, what you will: he had single-mindedness, and a Latin desire for clarity. What he achieved (and indeed it enriches every book he wrote) was a background devoid of insularity. He was proud of his adopted country, but from the very circumstances of his life, he saw her from without. No one has dwelt upon her with more affection. He would have been the first to appreciate the pleasing irony that the two writers who have written most perceptively about her seamen generally, and in particular of Nelson, should have been himself a Pole, and Alfred Mahan an American.

Oliver Warner thinks the readers of Conrad are invariably struck with his com-mand of language. To one who knew nothing of his origin, the thought would surely never occur that English was not his native tongue. Indeed his most persistent grammatical fault, the use of the word 'shall' where he intends 'will,' is a peculiarity common enough even in those to whom English is an inheritance.

How Conrad first learnt the language in which he wrote has been related. 'After hearing it spoken,' he told Mr. Megroz, and when I could talk enough, I read. I have a thick green-covered volume of Shakespeare I bought with my first earnings.' He learnt much from Mill's *Political Economy*, and from reading newspapers. Keats was his favourite English poet. Fennimore Cooper was known to his childhood from translations. In *Notes on Life* and *Letters* he says that, apart from his father's version of *The Two Gentlemen of Verona, Nicholas Nickleby* in Polish was his first introduction to English literature. He retained his affection for Dickens when he came to know the originals, particularly for *Bleak House*.

But it turns out that Jessie Conrad was doubly estranged by language when her new husband fell ill: She wrote in her work *Joseph Conrad as I Knew Him* "For a whole long week the fever ran high, and for most of the time Conrad was delirious. To see him lying in the white canopied bed, dark-faced, with gleaming teeth and shining eyes, was sufficiently alarming, but to hear him muttering to himself in a strange tongue (he must have been speaking Polish), to be unable to penetrate the clouded mind or catch one intelligible word, was for a young inexperienced girl truly awful."

This thumbnail sketch brings the man and the writer close in several ways. It anticipates a subject that Conrad would treat in 'Amy Foster,' a short story about the hostile reception afforded a Polish castaway in a Kentish village and turning upon a tragic linguistic misunderstanding between him and his English wife.

A second glimpse, this time from Ford Madox Ford, recalls Ford's early transactions with Conrad as a collaborator. He wrote in his *Joseph Conrad: A Personal Remembrance:* "His voice was then usually low, rather intimate and caressing. He began by speaking slowly but later on he spoke very fast. His accent was precisely, rather dusky, the accent of dark rather than fair races. He impressed the writer at first as a pure Marseilles Frenchman: he spoke English with great fluency and distinction, with correctitude in his syntax, his words absolutely exact as to meaning, but his accentuation so faulty that he was at times difficult to understand...He gesticulated with his hands and shoulders when he wished to be emphatic, but when he forgot himself in the excitement of talking he gesticulated with his whole body, throwing himself about in his chair, moving his chair nearer to yours. Finally he would spring up, go to a distance, and walk backwards and forwards across the end of the room."

Stressing the qualities of the hypersensitive or 'neurasthenic' personality noted by many others, Ford's observations provide further interesting clues as to why Conrad, as man and writer, is invariably thought to be 'elusive' and 'protean.'

Owen Knowles thinks the whole tenor of Conrad's life as Polish émigré and seaman seems to have encouraged in him habits of mind associated with what has later come to be identified as the hybrid 'marginal man' who, living 'in two worlds, in both of which he is a stranger,' needs self-consciously to fashion an identity from a medley of competing demands and allegiances.

Conrad and Great Writers

Joseph Conrad was a different and difficult writer compared to many great writers of the world. That way he is one of the unique writers in the world. Conrad was a Pole under Russian rule. He was a landed gentry's son but turned an orphan. He spoke Polish still learning Russian, French and English. He joined the French Navy but left it for the British Navy. Was not Conrad a seaman and captain? Yet he strived to become an English writer. He learnt English at his age of twenty-one, a great thing in itself. Conrad had many paradoxes still. Was Conrad a colonialist, an imperialist? It is difficult to say about it still though Chinua Achebe complains against him with anger. Did not Conrad write against the white man?

Conrad once began to write had a very good relationship with publishing agents and writers. Two important of them are Edward Garnett and J. B. Pinker. It was Garnett, the reader for the Fisher Unwin who helped Conrad to get his first novel *Almayer's*

Folly published in 1894. Edward Garnett is mission was to discover the genius and fight for his recognition. He discovered John Galsworthy, D.H. Lawrence, W.H. Davies, W.H. Hudson and H.E. Bates, and he was to be for a long time Conrad's friend and adviser. This reminds me George Meredith's helping Thomas Hardy get his fiction published by great publishing houses in London in the previous decades. Garentt's support for Conrad and his critical appreciation of his work was to outlast Conrad's life. Then there is Mr. J. B. Pinker, another book agent who furthered similar help to Conrad later.

Joseph Conrad's lengthy series of letters with James Brand Pinker, his literary agent from 1899 to 1922, is his true autobiography. Except for his sea career, this correspondence of over 1,200 items touches on virtually every aspect of Conrad's professional and private life, but is especially compelling in two major areas: first, his day-today personal life as he wrote his novels and stories; and second, the development of the fiction itself, the details of the slow, tortuous manner in which his literary work passed through his mind and pen.

Conrad and Schopenhauer

Arthur Schopenhauer's landmark book *The World as Will and Idea* (1819) seems to have influenced Conrad. The idea that the world itself is a malignant illusion is explicit in Conrad's fiction.

Schopenhauer (born Feb. 22, 1788, Danzig, Prussia-died Sept. 21,1860, Frankfurt am Main) was a German philosopher. His father was a banker and his mother a novelist. He studied in several fields before earning his doctorate in philosophy. He regarded the *Upanishads* together with the works of Plato and Kant, as the foundation of his philosophical system, a metaphysical doctrine of the will developed in reaction to the idealism of G. W. E Hegel. His magnum opus *The World as Will and Representation* (1819) consists of two comprehensive series of reflections on the theory of knowledge and the philosophy of nature, aesthetics and ethics. By turning away from spirit and reason to the powers of intuition, creativity, and the irrational, he influenced (partly via Nietzsche) the ideas and methods of vitalism, life philosophy, Existentialism, and anthropology. His other works include *On the Will in Nature* (1836), *The Two Main*

Problems of Ethics (1841), and *Parerga and Paralipomena* (1851). An unhappy and solitary man, his works earned him the sobriquet "the philosopher of pessimism."

Conrad and Nietzsche

Edward Said thinks Conrad and Nietzsche as Schopenhauer's followers loved to study life in its all manifestations. What troubled Nietzsche about Schopenhauer was the latter's weakening before the amoral picture of the world he had drawn. Whereas Nietzsche acknowledge life's uncompromising and inescapable disdain for either man or morality, he felt his once-revered teacher devised a cowardly retreat from life by preaching stoic withdrawal. Conrad's treatment of Heyst in *Victory*, whose code of philosophic disengagement from life is articulated only to be violated by Lena, Schomberg, Mr. Jones, and the others. These, plus a lifelong interest in Wagner, are part of a common cultural patrimony shared by Conrad and Nietzsche.

However, Conrad did not admire Nietzsche's assertion of the relativity of all values. His scepticism looks forward to the world picture of fragmentation, contingency, and provisionality that underlies the main Modernist writings of the 1920s.

Conrad and Rousseau

According to Zdzislaw Najder, Conrad's vision about man and society was influenced by Rousseau's thoughts of mankind. Najder Rather comparing Conrad with Rousseau is supposed to serve three purposes: firstly, to elucidate, by way of a contrastive analysis, Conrad's concepts of man and society; secondly, to place Conrad within the mainstream of European moral and socio-political thought which in turn, will make it possible to determine his position on the map of philosophical and political tendencies of his day; and finally to clarify the intellectual structure of those works of Conrad which can be interpreted in terms of his opposition to Rousseau's ideas.

The political issues raised in Conrad's fiction attracted scant notice during his lifetime. He was also gravely disappointed by lack of public response to 'Autocracy and War,' his longest piece of political journalism. But within the last thirty years Conrad as a political writer writer has been given a growing consideration.

Still, the conceptual framework of his thought, the sources and implications of his fundamental ideas of man, society, and historical process, and the relation of his beliefs to the main currents of European political philosophy have not been much expected.

Conrad and John Galsworthy, R.B. Cunninghame Graham and Ford Madox Ford

Conrad was well settled down in England by the year 1898. His wife was just pregnant of Borys. Edward Garnett, Galsworthy and Sanderson visited him often.

On his second voyage to Congo in 1890, the passengers included Edward Sanderson, son of the headmaster of Elstree Preparatory School, and John Galsworthy, then a very young man just down from Oxford. Galsworthy has left us his first impression of Conrad: "He was superintending the stowage of cargo. Very dark he looked in the burning sunlight, tanned, with a peaked brown beard, almost black hair, and dark brown eyes, over which the lids were deeply folded.... He spoke to me with a strong foreign accent. He seemed to me strange on an English ship.... Ever a great teller of a tale, he had already nearly twenty years of tales to tell. Tales of ships and storms, of Polish revolution, of youthful Carlist gun-running adventure, of the Malay seas, and the Congo." Both Galsworthy and Conrad remained life-long friends though intellectual differences persisted between them.

Even Conrad befriended Robert Cunninghame Graham, the adventurous and romantic descendant of King Robert II of Scotland, who also had Spanish and Italian blood in his veins. Graham had spent eight years in South America, ranching and living with gauchos, and had prospected for gold in Spain. He was at one time an MP (Liberal), involved in the Bloody Sunday demonstration in Trafalgar Square with William Morris, Bernard Shaw, Mrs Annie Besant and Prince Kropotkin. Conrad and Cunninghame Graham had this in common—they were both adventurers, they had both wandered over great parts of the globe, both were courageous journeyers. But politically they were far apart.

In September 1898, while staying with Edward Garnett, Conrad met Ford Madox Ford and seven years later such was the strength of their friendship that he was able to write to H.G. Wells: 'As to Ford he is a sort of lifelong habit.'

Ford Madox Ford (originally Hueffer), son of a famous music critic and related to both Ford Madox Brown, the painter, and William Michale Rossetti, was then twenty-four and already publishing. Wells described Ford as "a long blonde with a drawling manner...What he is really or if he is really, nobody knows now and he least of all; he has become a great system of assumed persons and dramatized selves.'

In course of time, Ford suggested that the Conrads should rent from him Pent Farm, an old farmhouse at Stanford, near Hythe in south-west Kent, and as Conrad liked it immediately, they moved in at beginning of autumn. The two wrote the novels *The Inheritors—an Extravagant Story* (1901) and *Romance—a Novel* (1903). Conrad had been disturbed at the lack of general popularity of his earlier work, and the very theme of *The Inheritors* suggests it. The hero of the story is, as was Conrad and, indeed, Hueffer at the time, an obscure writer of integrity. He meets a strange girl in Canterbury, who tells him she belongs to the Fourth Dimension. By her instrumentality he is whirled into an atmosphere of success as a journalist; he becomes acquainted with high finance; he collaborates in a book on Cromwell with the Foreign Secretary (whose name by the way is Churchill); he falls in love with his Fourth Dimensional lady, and the end of the story is financial crash, suicides, the fall of Churchill, and the return of the writer to a different kind of obscurity. *The Inheritors* exposes popular writers, journalists, politicians, high finance, publishers, everything it touches except the honest craftsman. It contains certain timeless lessons, and the vitality of the story is unquestionable.

In *The Inheritors*, whose title is explained by the fact that the Fourth Dimensional people, with a genius for power, were to inherit the earth. Conrad had strayed to London and Paris. There is no breath of the East, or the sea. In *Romance*, on the other hand, the collaborators drew to the full on Conrad's early experiences of the Caribbean. It is a long book, and for sustained excitement has few superiors in its genre. Action is continuous, the romance between the hero, John Kemp, and the aristocratic Spanish Seraphina, is both tender, chivalrous and, within its particular rather porcelain convention, convincing, while in their friend Castro, Crevoni undoubtedly appears once more. Packed with action, it contains an ample picture of the true squalor of piracy, and of the Caribbean in the early years of the nineteenth century. More than this, the enmity between Kemp and O'Brien, the principal protagonists, is made to symbolize the eternal distrust of the Irish for the English, the Catholic for the heretic, the outcast for the established. The novel depicts the clash between the two.

Oliver Warner observes, "Since Conrad's day there has been increasing taste for stories of this kind, perfectly adapted as they are for the cinematograph. That *Romance* did not sell widely when it first appeared does not reflect on the craftsmanship which went to the making of it. This was masterly. Madox Hueffer, with characteristic exaggeration, used to say that he taught Conrad to write. It was not true; but Conrad gained from the collaborations, and they were, indeed, the immediate precursors of his greatest imaginative effort, *Nostromo* (1904)."

Ford claims that he and Conrad believed that 'a novel should be the biography of a man or of an affair, and a biography...should be a novel'. The distinguishing feature of Ford's particular book is that in it we have 'a projection of Joseph Conrad as, little by little, he revealed himself to a human being during many years of close intimacy. It is so that, by degree, Lord Jim appeared to Marlowe or that every human soul by degrees appears to every other human soul.' Ford tries to illustrate the growth of his acquaintance with Conrad and, by doing so, to make Conrad more graphically present to the reader. But he does not do so by means of a narration. Ford means a sequential account of surface events. His starting point and his fictional unit is an impression, and he describes his book as 'the writer's impression of a writer who avowed himself impressionist.

Conrad, Dickens and Hardy

Conrad loved to read specially English and French literatures. When young his father asked him to read Shakespeare's plays and Hugo's poetry.

In 1869 the 12 year-old orphan Joseph was placed under the guardianship of his maternal uncle Thaddeus Bobrowski in Krakow, Poland. The lonely and unhappy boy read a great deal.

The stories of Frederick Marryat and Charles Dickens roused his interests. Victor Hugo's *Les Travailleurs* roused his interest in the sea. He studied under a tutor Adam Pulman and he went abroad with him.

Conrad, like Kafka, read Dickens greatly. In fact, he said he modeled his novel *The Secret Agent* on Dickens's *Bleak House* (1853) Dickens's father was an irresponsible clerk, and Dickens had to work as a child laborer. Then Dickens became a journalist and writer. He emerged a great social critic of Victorian England. His great novels are *Oliver Twist* (1839), *Dombey and Son* (1848), *David Copperfield* (1850), *Bleak House* (1853), *Hard Times* (1854), *A Tale of Two Cities* (1859) and *Great Expectations*. Dickens had an interest in social problems; capital punishment, the reform of prostitutes and the like. So prolific was his output and so frenzied his life, it seems miraculous he lived as long as he did.

Norman Page observes, "In its evocation of the squalor and brutality of lower-class life in the metropolis, *The Secret Agent* owes something to Dickens, and in its combination of this element with a story of espionage and political intrigue it represents the side of Conrad that was to be an important influence on Graham Greene."

Conrad had an unsual interest in Napolonic wars. Like Thomas Hardy whom he succedded as a great English novelist, Conrad wrote the novel *Suspense* based on this theme. In 1920 he began what was to be his last work *Suspense*, a Napoleonic novel, and in January 1921, went with Jessie to Corsica, staying in Ajaccio, where he did some background reading for the novel. But Corsica was 'Cold. Wet, Horrors.' Conrad has written some stories on this theme.

Conrad was like his Jim. He found much rootlessness in his life. He had this displacement that he left his country and found out a citizenship of England. Hence, he remained loyal to that great seafaring nation.

As with persons, so with nations. Conrad believed in England's fidelity. It was one of the reasons for his respect. He said that Europe had needed of her. When he visited Poland just before the first World War, he tells us in *Notes on Life and Letters*, he was asked to prognosticate the behaviour of this country. He was at first reluctant to do so, but said at length: 'If England comes into the war, then, no matter who may want to make peace at the end of six months at the cost of right and justice, England will keep on fighting for years if necessary, you may reckon on that."

Inspired or not, he was right, for two reasons; the first was that he never lost sight of the moral issue in men and affairs—indeed, it was to him the cardinal factor; the second was because he had studied history, particularly that of the era of Napoleon. From that age he, like Hardy in *The Dynasts,* and many other writers, had sought and found lessons of permanent validity. He had that rare gift, political acuteness, based both upon intuition and long observation. It is revealed most often in asides, as when, for instance, in *The Mirror of the Sea,* he says: 'In the policy of winds, as amongst the tribes of the earth, the real struggle lies between east and west.'

Conrad's Vision of Life

Conrad's was a Western mind, strongly infused with Latin individuality, with an English awareness of moral issues, and a sense of form rare in writers of fiction. If, as seems likely, the best of his work has lasting vitality, it will surely be for these characteristics. He would be a pessimist indeed who thought their value ephemeral.

Conrad was and is appreciated enough for his life and works. Virginia Woolf, for instance, in *The Common Reader* (1925) thought that it was *Youth, Lord Jim, Typhoon, The Nigger of the ' Narcissus'* 'We shall re-read in their entirety.' Later assessment would amplify her choice, though no critic has bettered her tribute to his work in general. ' One opens his pages', she wrote, 'and feels as Helen must have felt when she looked in her glass and realized that, do what she would, she could never in any circumstances pass for a plain woman.'

Conrad's pessimism as to mankind's condition was complete, and its influence in his work was not conducive to popularity: 'what makes mankind tragic is not that they are the victims of nature, it is that they are conscious of it. But as soon as you know of your slavery the pain, the anger, the strife—the tragedy begins.' He graphically explained his view of the universe in a letter to Cunninghame Graham: "There is a– let us say–machine. It evolved itself...out of a chaos of scraps of iron and behold!—it knits. I am horrified at the horrible work and stand appalled. I feel it ought to embroider–but it goes on knitting.... You cannot by any special lubrication make embroidery with a knitting machine. And the most withering thought is that the infamous thing has made itself; made itself without thought, without conscience, without foresight, without eyes, without heart.... It knits us in and it knits us out. It has knitted time, space, pain, death, corruption, despair and the illusions– and nothing matters. I'll admit however that to look at the remorseless process is sometimes amusing."

It is not surprising that Bertrand Russell (who met Conrad first in 1913) said of him, 'I felt...that he though of civilized and morally tolerable human life as a dangerous walk on a thin crust of barely cooled lava which at any moment might break and let the unwary sink into fiery depths.'

Annexure

Chronology of Conrad's Life

1857 Jozef Teodor Konrad Korzenioski, only child of poet, dramatist, translator and political activist, Apollo Korzenioski and Ewelina, nee Bobrowska, born on 3 December in or near Berdichov in the Ukraine.

1861 Apollo Korzenioski arrested and imprisoned in Warsaw for anti-Russian conspiracy.

1862 The Korzenioskis are exiled to Vologda, northern Russia.

1865 Death of Ewa Korzenioski.

1868 Apollo Korzenioski and his son move to Lwow.

1869 Death of Apollo Korzenioski in Cracow. Maternal uncle, Tadeusz Bobrowski, becomes young Korzenioski's guardian. Privately tutored because of ill health, also occasionally attends schools during the next few years.

1873 Visits Austria, Germany, Switzerland and northern Italy with his tutor Adam Pulman.

1874 Leaves Poland for Marseilles to become a trainee seaman in the French Merchant Service. Works for shippers and bankers Delestang et Fils.

1874-7 Passenger and apprentice in the *Mont-Blanc* and 'steward' in the *Saint-Antonine* (to the Caribbean).

1978 Shoots himself in the chest in Marseilles after accumulating gambling debts but escapes serious injury. Joins the steamship *Movis,* his first British ship. Serves as ordinary seaman in the *Skimmer of the Sea*.

1878-80	Ordinary seaman in the *Duke of Sutherland* (to Australia) and in the steamship *Europe* (Mediterranean).
1880	Passes examination for second mate. Third mate in the *Loch Etive* (to Australia).
1881-4	Second mate in the *Palestine, Riversdale,* and *Narcissus* (to South-East Asia and India).
1884	Passes examination for first mate.
1885-6	Second mate in the *Tilkhurst* (to Singapore and Calcutta).
1886	Becomes a British subject. Passes examination for master's certificate.
1886-7	Second mate in the *Falconhurst.* First mate in the *Highland Forest* (to Java). Injured on board, is hospitalized in Singapore.
1887-8	First mate in the steamship *Vidar* (from Singapore to various Netherlands East Indies ports).
1888	Master of the *Otago,* joined in Bangkok, sails to Australia and Mauritius.
1889	Resigns from the *Otago.* Settles briefly in London and begins *Almayer's Folly.*
1890	Friendship with marriage relation and writer Marguerite Poradowska. In the Congo Free State for the Societe pour le Commerce du Haut-Congo as second in command and, temporarily, captain of the river steamer *Rot des Beiges.*
1891	Manages the warehouse of Barr, Moering in London.
1891-3	First mate in the passenger clipper *Torrens* (to Australia).
	Meets John Galsworthy, among her passengers. Visits Bobrowski in the Ukraine.
1894	*Almayer's Folly* accepted for publication. Meets Edward Garnett, publisher's reader, and Jessie George, a typist, whom he later marries. Signs on as second mate in the *Adowa* but sails only to France and back. End of his sea career.

1895	*Almayer's Folly* published under the pen name 'Joseph Conrad.'
1896	*An Outcast of the Islands* published. Marries Jessie George (24 March) and honeymoons in Brittany. Begins *The Rescuer.*
	Settles in Stanford-le-Hope, Essex. Becomes acquainted with H.G. Wells and initiates a correspondence with Henry James.
1897	Begins friendships with writer and political figure R. B. Cunninghame Graham and with Stephen Crane. *The Nigger of the 'Narcissus'* published.
1898	Son Borys born. *Tales of Unrest* published ('Karain,' 'The Idiots,' 'An Outpost of Progress,' 'The Return,' 'The Lagoon'). Collaborates with Ford Madox Ford and takes over from him lease of The Pent, Postling, Kent.
1899	*Heart of Darkness* serialized.
1899-1900	*Lord Jim* serialized.
1900	In Belgium with Ford. J. B. Pinker becomes Conrad's agent. *Lord Jim* published in book form.
1901	*The Inheritors* (collaboration with Ford) published.
1902	*Youth: A Narrative; and Two Other Stories* published ('Youth,' *Heart of Darkness,* 'The End of the Tether').
1903	*Typhoon and Other Stories* ('Typhoon,' 'Amy Foster,' Talk,' 'To-morrow') and *Romance* (collaboration with Ford) published.
1904	*Nostromo* serialized and published in book form. Jessie Conrad injures her knees, remaining partially disabled for life.
1905	Sojourn on Capri. *One Day More,* dramatization of 'To-morrow,' staged in London.
1906	Sojourn in Montpellier. Son John born. *The Mirror of the Sea* published. *The Secret Agent* serialized in US.
1907	Sojourn in Montpellier and in Geneva. *The Secret Agent* published in book form. Moves to Someries, Luton Hoo, Bedfordshire.

1908	*A Set of Six* published ('Caspar Ruiz,' 'The Informer,' The Brute,' 'An Anarchist,' The Duel,' 'Il Conde').
1909	Moves to Aldington, Kent. Breaks with Ford.
1910	Completes *Under Western Eyes* and suffers a nervous break-down. Moves to Capel House, Orlestone, Kent.
1910-11	*Under Western Eyes* serialized and published in book form.
1912	*Some Reminiscences* (later A *Personal Record)* and *'Twixt Land and Sea* published ('A Smile of Fortune,' 'The Secret Sharer,' 'Freya of the Seven Isles'). *Chance* serialized in New York.
1914	*Chance* published in book form. First financial success. Visits Poland in summer[1] with family. Trapped for some weeks by the outbreak of war, returns to England via Austria and Italy.
1915	*Within the Tides* ('The Planter of Malata,' 'The Partnerm' 'The Inn of the Two Witches,' 'Because of the Dollars') and *Victory* published.
1917	*The Shadow-Line* published.
1919	Moves to Spring Grove, near Wye, Kent. Basil Macdonald Hastings's dramatization of *Victory* staged in London. Moves to Oswalds, Bishopsbourne, near Canterbury. *The Arrow of Gold* published. Begins 'Author's Notes' for Doubleday and Heinemann Collected Editions.
1920	*The Rescue,* begun in 1898, published.
1921	Visits Corsica, doing research for *The Rover* and *Suspense.* *Notes on Life and Letters* published. Collected Editions begin publication.
1922	Dramatization of *The Secret Agent* staged in London.
1923	Visits the United States to a rapturous reception. *The Rover* serialized in US and published in book form.

1924	Declines a knighthood. Dies of a heart attack at Oswalds on 3 August, aged 66. Buried in Roman Catholic section of Canterbury cemetery. *The Nature of a Crime* (collaboration with Ford) published in book form.
1925	*Tales of Hearsay* ('The Warrior's Soul,' 'Prince Roman,' 'The Tale,' 'The Black Mate') and *Suspense* published.
1926	*Last Essays,* edited by Richard Curie, published.
1928	*The Sisters* (fragment) published.

Select Bibliography

Joseph Conrad's Works

Novels

Almayer's Folly (1895)
An Outcast of the Islands (1896)
The Nigger of the 'Narcissus' (1897)
Heart of Darkness (1902)
Lord Jim (1900)
Typhoon (1903)
Nostromo (1904)
The Secret Agent (1907)
Under the Western Eyes (1911)
Freya of the Seven Isles (1902)
Chance (1913)
Victory (1915)
The Shadow Line (1917)
The Arrow of Gold (1919)
The Rescue (1920)
The Rover (1923)
Suspense (1925)
The Sisters (1928)

Short Stories

Tales of Unrest (1898)
Youth: A Narrative and Two Other Stories (1902)
Typhoon and Other Stories (1902)
A Set of Six (1908)

'Twist Land and Sea (1912)

Within the Tides (1915)

Tales of Hearsay (1925)

Others

The Mirror of the Sea (1906)

A Personal Record

Works on Joseph Conrad

Alien, Jerry. *The Sea Years of Joseph Conrad.* New York, 1965.

Baines, Jocelyn. *Joseph Conrad: A Critical Biography.* New York: McGraw-Hill, 1960.

Berman, Jeffrey. Joseph *Conrad: Writing as Rescue.* New York: Astra, 1977.

Blackburn, William, ed. *Joseph Conrad: Letters to William Blackwood and David S.* Meldrum. Durham, N.C., 1958.

Bradbrook, M. C. *Joseph Conrad: Poland's English Genius.* Cambridge: Cambridge University Press, 1941.

Bruce, ed. *Conrad's Heart of Darkness and the Critics.* Belmont, Calif.: Wadsworth, 1960.

Conrad, Borys. *My Father: Joseph Conrad.* New York, 1970.

_____________ *Coach Tour of Joseph Conrad's Homes in Kent. Joseph Conrad Society pamphlet,* 1974.

Conrad, Jessie. *Joseph Conrad As I Knew Him.* London, 1916. *Joseph Conrad and His Circle.* London, 1935.

Conrad, John. *Joseph Conrad: Times Remembered.* Cambridge, 1981.

Conrad, Joseph. *Letters to His Wife.* Preface by Jessie Conrad Korzeniowska. Lon-don, 1927.

Curie, Richard. *Joseph Conrad: A Study.* London, 1914.

_____________ . *The Last Twelve Years of Joseph Conrad.* London, 1928.

Daleski, H. M. *Joseph Conrad: The Way of Dispossession.* London: Faber & Faber, 1977.

Danilewiczowa, Maria, ed. *Joseph Conrad:* London, 1957.

Davis, Harold E. "Conrad's Revision of *The Secret Agent*: A Study."

Ehrsam, T. G. *A Bibliography of Conrad.* Metuchen, N.J.: Scarecrow, i969.

Fogel, Aaron. *Coercion to Speak: Conrad's Poetics of Dialogue.* Cambridge: Harvard University Press, 1965.

Farjeon, Eleanor.Edward Thomas: *The Last Four Years.* London, 1958.

Follett, Wilson. *Joseph Conrad: A Short Study of His Intellectual and Emotional Attitude Toward His Work and of the Chief Characteristics of His Novels.* Garden City, N.Y., 1915.

Ford, Ford Madox. Joseph Conrad: *A Personal Remembrance.* London, 1934.

Gillon, Adam. *Joseph Conrad.* Boston: Twayne, 1982.

Glassman, Peter J. *Language and Being: Joseph Conrad and the Literature of Personality.* New York: Columbia University Press, 1976.

Guerard, Albert J. *Conrad the Novelist.* Cambridge: Harvard University Press, 1958.

Galsworthy, John.*Castles in Spain.* New York, 1927.

Garnett, Edward, ed. *Letters from Conrad:*1895 to 1924. London, 1928.

______________, ed. *Letters from John Galsworthy.* Saint Clair Shores, Minn., 1971.

Gee, John A., and Sturm, Paul J., eds. *Letters of Joseph Conrad to Marguerite Poradowska.* New Haven, Conn., 1940.

Gordan, John D. *Joseph Conrad: The Making of a Novelist.* Cambridge, Mass., 1940.

Hay, Eloise K. *The Political Novels of Joseph Conrad.* Chicago, 1963.

Hewitt, Douglas. *Conrad: A Reassessment.* Cambridge, 1951.

Johnson, Bruce M. *Conrad's Models of Mind.* Minneapolis: University of Minnesota Press, 1971.

Karl, Frederick R. *A Reader's Guide to Joseph Conrad.* New York, 1969.

Keating, George T., ed. *A Conrad Memorial Library*: The Collection of George T. Keating. Garden City, N.Y., 1929.

Kirschner, Paul. *Conrad: The Psychologist as Artist.* Edinburgh, 1968.

Krzyzanowski, Ludwik., ed. *Joseph Conrad: Centennial Essays.* New York, 1960.

Kirschner, Robert. *Heart of Darkness: The Psychologist as Artist.* Edinburgh: Oliver & Boyd, 1968.

Leavis, F. R. *The Great Tradition: George Eliot, Henry James, Joseph Conrad.* New York: New York University Press, 1963.

McLauchlan, Juliet. "The 'Value' and 'Significance' *of Heart of Darkness." Conradian* 15 (1983): 3-21.

Meyer, Bernard C. *Joseph Conrad: A Psychoanalytic Biography.* Princeton: Princeton University Press, 1967.

Parry, Benita. *Conrad's Imperialism.* Englewood Cliffs, N.J.: Salem, 1984.

Mudrick, Marvin, ed. *Conrad: A Collection of Critical Essays.* Englewood Cliffs, N.J.: Prentice-Hall, 1966.

Nettels, Elsa. *James and Conrad.* Athens, Ga., 1977.

Palmer, John A. *Joseph Conrad's Fiction: A Study in Literary Growth.* Ithaca, N.Y.: Cornell University Press, 1968.

Said, Edward W. *Joseph Conrad and the Fiction of Autobiography.* Cambridge: Harvard University Press, 1966.

Sherry, Norman. *Conrad's Eastern World.* Cambridge, 1966.

______________ . *Conrad's Western World.* Cambridge, 1971.

______________ , ed. *Conrad: The Critical Heritage.* London, 1973.

______________ , ed. *Joseph Conrad: A Commemoration.* London, 1976.

Sutherland, J. G. *At Sea with Joseph Conrad.* Boston, 1911.

Stallman, Robert W., ed. *The Art of Joseph Conrad: A Critical Symposium.* East Lansing: Michigan State University Press, 1960.

Tennant, Roger. *Joseph Conrad: A Biography.* New York: Atheneum, 1981.

Thornburn, David. *Conrad's Romanticism.* New Haven: Yale University Press, 1974.